The San Francisco
Dinner Party Cookbook

A SAN FRANCISCO BOOK COMPANY/HOUGHTON MIFFLIN BOOK

Houghton Mifflin Company   Boston   1975

The San Francisco Dinner Party Cookbook

JUDITH ETS-HOKIN

Illustrations by Meredith Wilson

V 10 9 8 7 6 5 4 3 2 1

Library of Congress Cataloging in Publication Data

Ets-Hokin, Judith.
  The San Francisco dinner party cookbook.

  "A San Francisco Book Company/Houghton Mifflin book."
  Includes index.
  1. Dinners and dining. 2. Menus. 3. Cookery.
  I. Title.
  TX737.E87   641.5'68   74-30116
  ISBN 0-913374-18-0
  ISBN 0-395-20287-6

Printed in the United States of America

This SAN FRANCISCO BOOK COMPANY/ HOUGHTON MIFFLIN BOOK originated in San Francisco and was produced and published jointly. Distribution is by Houghton Mifflin Company, 2 Park Street, Boston, Massachusetts 02107.

Contents

Foreword

WHEN I MARRIED fourteen years ago, I knew very little about cooking and entertaining. I liked to cook and felt confident in the kitchen with my family, but I was not comfortable entertaining guests in the dining room.

I had too many unanswered questions. How many people should I entertain at one time? What wines should I serve? What kinds of dishes go well together on a menu? What is the best way to serve a meal? And most important, how could I cook dinner and be with my guests at the same time?

While I was wondering where to begin, a friend called and invited me to attend with her a series of cooking classes offered by Monsieur Paul Quiaud, chef of Ernie's Restaurant in San Francisco. It was a timely opportunity.

As I observed and worked and tasted, a new world opened to me, one of infinite pleasures and excitement. I learned that there is always a new food to taste, a new dish to sample, a new combination of flavors to create.

For some years following, I attended a variety of cooking classes. I began to understand more fully what happens when ingredients are combined and cooked and what foods complement each other, as well as which are contrary to one another.

Gradually I began entertaining close friends. Soon I was entertaining often and answering for myself, by trial and error, those questions about cooking and entertaining that had at one time so overwhelmed me.

Friends began asking me for methods and recipes. Everyone was interested in dinner party menus that could be prepared ahead. Finally, a neighbor organized a group

of ten people into my first cooking class where I demonstrated complete menus that could be prepared in advance.
In a short time, my classes grew to five a week.

In the menus following, I have attempted to answer
many of the questions that I found so difficult in the past.
All the menus and methods have been demonstrated in
my cooking classes and have been served to many guests
in my home.

It is hoped that this book will offer a wide range of
alternatives to the standard American company menu of
roast beef and green beans with almonds, as well as aiding
the host or hostess who wants to provide the best for his
guests, graciously and with ease.

Acknowledgments

My deepest appreciation to LAUREL FEIGENBAUM *for her help and to* SANDOR BURSTEIN *for his thoughtful wine suggestions. And to my children,* REBECCA, SOLOMON, *and* GABRIEL, *for their patience.*

A Word on Entertaining and Advance Preparation

ENTERTAINING people at dinner in your home is a little like the art of creating a theatrical production. In a play, all the major elements are coordinated by the director, who makes sure the lines spoken by the actors, the set, the lighting, the costumes, the music are at their best and in harmony with one another—which is just the sort of coordinating the host or hostess entertaining at home must do.

Once you have chosen a date and invited a group of compatible guests, the menu must be selected, the shopping done, the wines chosen, the table set, and finally the meal prepared and served. Assuming—as almost everyone does these days—that you are to be bartender, butler, cook, and waiter, there is the necessity to plan well. How can you make sure your "production" will be a success?

First, if you want to have your guests seated and served at table, don't attempt more than eight people at a time. Six is ideal. When selecting a menu, always consider the tastes of your guests. If there is any doubt that all of them will like kidneys, for example, it is best to choose something else.

After a menu is selected, read through the shopping list and ask yourself if all the ingredients are in season and readily available. Then read the recipes carefully. Do you have all the necessary serving and cooking utensils or reasonable substitutes at hand? Do you understand all the cooking terms and recipe instructions? (Once, some years ago, I was assembling a recipe for chocolate mousse which called for two teaspoons of coffee to be added to the melting chocolate. That seemed odd to me, but after rereading it several times I decided that's what it definitely said, so I added two teaspoons of ground coffee. Later on, when I served the mousse, my guests wanted to know what coffee grounds were doing in a mousse. I suddenly realized that the recipe meant coffee in its liquid form.)

Always complete your grocery shopping at least a day in advance, leaving only highly perishable foods like fish to be purchased on the day of the party.

The evening or morning before dinner, set the table completely. Set out in the kitchen all the dishes, including the coffee cups, saucers, and serving dishes you will be using, ready to be warmed or placed on the table as needed. Check the liquor, mixes, wines, and ice. When all of this has been accomplished, prepare any recipes that require thorough chilling.

Next, do all the advance preparation possible for the rest of the meal, like chopping vegetables, shelling nuts, grating lemon peel, etc. Cover these and store in the refrigerator or on the counter top until needed.

At this point of preparation you will need approximately two hours more to finish most of the menus in this book. This may be done during the day or the two hours before your guests are due to arrive, depending upon your schedule. I do the last of the meal preparation while I'm feeding the children around five in the afternoon, finishing by seven, which leaves me time to freshen up. Since I have three small children who must be attended to, I rarely invite people for dinner earlier than 7:30 P.M.

A word about children and pets. After a brief greeting to your guests, let the children, if possible, amuse themselves in their own rooms, not in the living and dining rooms. Your guests should be relaxed and undisturbed by little cowboys and Indians, or by a child demanding a bedtime story. Put pets out of the way as well; not everyone enjoys a dog on the lap or a begging animal under the dinner table.

To save yourself from dishwashing at midnight, if at all possible arrange with your own teen-age child or a neighborhood girl or boy to help you that evening with the younger children, the final clearing of the table, and the dishwashing. Whenever I am unable to have that little extra help, I serve coffee in the living room and never attempt to clear the table or tidy up the kitchen while my guests are present.

At seven-thirty, I light the candles and make a last-minute check of the living and dining rooms. When my guests arrive, I am ready for them.

Memo to the Cook

THE FOLLOWING are certain food or cooking terms that may need further explanation, and some suggestions for serving.

Butter

WITHOUT EXCEPTION, the butter used in the recipes throughout this book is unsalted. You may keep unsalted butter in the freezer for months (out of the freezer it turns rancid quickly), removing a cube at a time as you need it. The difference in flavor is beyond comparison.

Coffee

UNLESS ONE or more guests prefer coffee with their food, I serve coffee as a separate course at the end of a meal, most often in the living room. My favorite after-dinner coffee is a dark French roast, blended equally with a lighter Italian roast. I purchase the coffee beans and then grind them as needed in a small electric grinder, using the drip method of pouring boiling water over the blend and letting the coffee drip through a filter into a server, to be served immediately.

Consistency of Sauces

IN THE RECIPES following, I often write about cooking a sauce down to the "right consistency." In those instances the only way to determine whether or not a sauce is right is for the cook to look at it, perhaps put a spoon through it, and determine by its thickness or thinness whether or not it is the 'right consistency' for that particular dish. By boiling or cooking a sauce longer, you reduce the liquid, concentrate the flavor, and thicken it by allowing the steam to evaporate. You thin a sauce by adding liquid.

Homemade Stocks

A FRESH, homemade stock is the secret ingredient of many fine dishes and sauces. Canned stocks cannot compare in flavor. I save all the bones and scraps of uncooked meat in plastic bags in the freezer, taking care to keep beef, veal, chicken, and lamb separate. When I have an adequate amount of meat and bones, I make stock (see pages 158, 159, 164). It is easy to do and worth the effort.

Hors d'Oeuvre

EACH MENU in this book is designed to provide a complete meal. Should you wish, however, to serve cocktails before dinner, an accompaniment is usually served.

I often serve the first course of a menu in the living room with cocktails. Should you decide to do this, be sure to announce that it is the first course of dinner, so that your guests won't "save" their appetites for later.

An alternative is a small, attractively arranged assortment of such things as pepperoncini, stuffed olives, pickled onions, tiny marinated mushrooms and artichokes, and perhaps some marinated herring. Another possibility is an arrangement of chilled raw vegetables with a bowl of sour cream or mayonnaise into which they may be dipped. All of these may be arranged hours ahead, perhaps on a partitioned dish, covered and chilled until time to serve.

Sometimes, a well-aged, unchilled Camembert or Brie cheese with biscuits and unsalted butter may be served.

Above all, it is most important not to extend your cocktail hour. A two- to three-hour cocktail period with lots

xvi

of hors d'oeuvre is a meal in itself, and dinner is no longer anticipated. On the other hand, two or three hours of cocktails without hors d'oeuvre numbs the palate and consequently your guests' enjoyment of the meal.

Keeping Food Warm

OFTEN A recipe requires that a dish be "kept warm" or be "put in a warm place" until time to serve. Of course there is no problem, if, like a friend of mine, you have an appliance that is a food warmer. Most of us, however, must improvise. I have an open grill on one side of my stove that is always warm because of the pilot light. That is where the food, lightly covered with foil, usually goes to stay warm. Sometimes, the dish may remain on the stove over a still warm but turned-off burner, or in a pot over hot water, or, in certain cases, in an oven that is on low or still warm after being turned off. How and where to keep food warm is something you have to decide according to the arrangement of your own kitchen.

Reheating

I HAVE FOUND that certain vegetables, sauces, meats, fish, and poultry reheat nicely as long as they are not refrigerated between the original cooking and the reheating. Follow the specific suggestions in each menu as to whether a rapid or slow reheating is required.

Seasonings

WHEN PREPARING many of the dishes in this book, I double and sometimes triple the amount of seasonings specified. Taste is a personal matter, and my taste for highly seasoned dishes may not be precisely yours. I have attempted to allow for this by indicating "season to taste" or "adjust seasonings" or "use 1 to 3 tablespoons."

You are the cook, so season to your own taste and let your individuality prevail.

Service

IN PRESENTING a meal, let the type of service depend partly on the menu and partly on how many guests are expected.

If you choose a buffet-style service, by all means provide the diners with a table at which to sit. The only exception is a large buffet with a menu that does not require a knife.

Should you want a slightly more formal presentation, bring the warmed plates to the table along with the dishes to be served. This type of service requires attractive cooking-serving containers. Serve each plate yourself and ask the guests to pass them.

A third possibility is to serve from the kitchen. With hot foods, you will probably need some assistance with this type of service so that the plates can be brought to the dining room as soon as they are served.

In any case, provide small portions instead of large ones, offering second helpings if desired. I always ask my guests to begin eating as soon as they are served with hot food. No matter what kind of service you choose, make sure the plates are always warmed for hot dishes.

Don't attempt to have an absolutely formal meal where no one passes a plate or leaves the table. It is unnecessary to try to emulate the service of a luxury restaurant in your home.

Substitutions

THE MENUS and recipes that follow are complete. They need no more ingredients than are specified. This does not mean, on the other hand, that they are untouchable.

Again, according to personal taste one or two ingredients may be added or omitted with no harm done. Substituting one vegetable for another, one fruit for another, or interchanging different kinds of fish or substituting capon for chicken is the way in which new dishes are created. Substituting for preference will give you infinite variety.

You cannot, however, substitute margarine for butter, frozen or canned fruit and vegetables for fresh, or canned creamed soup for sauces and expect results even close to those using specified ingredients.

"Until Done"

THE PHRASE "until done" refers to vegetables that are just barely tender, braised meats that are tender and browned, grilled or roasted meats that are cooked to the desired degree of doneness—for poultry, when the joints move easily, and for fish, when the flesh turns whitely opaque. Cakes are done when they barely begin to shrink back from the sides of the pan or when a toothpick inserted into the center of the cake comes out clean. Custards are done when a stainless-steel knife inserted into the center comes out clean.

Wines

GOOD WINE enhances the pleasure of a good dinner. Therefore it is necessary to plan the wines served with a meal as an integral part of the menu.

Any wine with a taste that is harmonious with the food it accompanies is the right wine for that food and for you. There are, nevertheless, certain traditions that are worth noting because they represent the cumulative experience of many wine drinkers of many tastes.

Generally speaking, do not serve full-bodied red wines with delicate chicken, fish, or veal dishes. By the same token, a delicate dry white wine is lost when served with a highly seasoned beef dish. If the main dish is cooked in wine, it is logical to drink more of the same wine with it.

A red wine should be in the house at least one day

before it is to be served, to give it a chance to rest, and it should be opened and placed on the dinner table an hour or so before dinner. White wines should be served thoroughly chilled.

Sweet wines may be served with dessert, and brandies and liqueurs are pleasant with coffee or following a meal. They complete the mood of easy, graceful elegance, but of course they are not absolutely necessary.

Specific wine suggestions accompany each of the menus in this book.

Author's Note

BEFORE ATTEMPTING any dish in this book, please read through the entire recipe in advance of preparation, as oftentimes the dish may need to stand or marinate for some time before serving.

The shopping lists following each menu are divided into two sections. In the section titled "shopping list" are mostly fresh ingredients needed specifically for the dishes in that menu. The "staples" section lists needed items that you most likely have on hand but may wish to check before going shopping.

Light Suppers

Crêpes Louise

Watercress and Endive Salad

Fresh Fruit Compote

Coconut Macaroons

TO SERVE 6

WINE
*A French Vouvray or a
Maryland White.*

REMARKS

THIS LITTLE dinner is a perfect before- or after-theater meal. It is rich and elegant, you do not need a lot of time to consume it, and it is quick and easy to prepare as well as simple to serve. A warmed loaf of French bread and butter is a nice addition.

METHOD

PREPARE the crêpes well ahead. Have the salad crisping in the refrigerator, the fruit chilling in its serving bowl. Bake the macaroons in advance and have them waiting on a serving plate. An hour or so before the guests arrive, make the crab filling, fill the crêpes, and place them in an attractive baking dish. Ten minutes before serving put them into the oven, and serve them at the table from the baking dish. A watercress and endive salad with mustard dressing is suggested.

Should you wish to serve dinner after the theater, assemble the crêpes before you go out, refrigerate them in their baking dish, then double the baking time.

Crêpes Louise

PREPARE twelve 7-inch crêpes (see Basic Recipe, page 160).

For the filling, sauté 6 finely chopped shallots in 3 tablespoons unsalted butter and add ¾ pound cooked crab meat. Add 2 beaten egg yolks and 1 tablespoon Madeira to 1½ cups béchamel sauce (see below). Reserve ½ cup of the sauce and add the crab meat and shallot mixture to the remaining sauce.

Spread crêpes with the crab meat filling. Roll them and arrange on a buttered ovenproof serving dish, covering the crêpes with the reserved béchamel sauce. Cover with

4

foil and warm in a 350-degree oven for about 10 minutes. If desired, glaze under the broiler for a few seconds just before serving.

Béchamel Sauce

IN A SAUCEPAN melt 4 tablespoons butter, stir in 4 tablespoons flour, and cook 1 minute over a low flame, without letting the mixture take on any color. Add 1½ cups light cream little by little, until the sauce reaches the right consistency (page xv), a bit thicker than heavy cream.

Salad

WATERCRESS and endive, with mustard dressing (see Basic Recipes, page 162).

Fresh Fruit Compote

SELECT any fruit or combination of fruits, such as strawberries, raspberries, blueberries, plums, peaches, pears, apples, bananas, figs, grapes, etc. Wash the chosen fruits, drain, cut uniformly, and sweeten to taste with finely granulated sugar. Flavor with 3 to 4 tablespoons Kirsch, or any fruit brandy. Blend well, cover the dish, and let the fruit mellow in the refrigerator.

Coconut Macaroons

BEAT 4 egg whites stiff. Add a teaspoon of vanilla, gradually beat in 1 cup confectioners' sugar, and continue beating until the mixture is stiff and glossy. Fold in ½ cup flour and 2 cups shredded coconut. Drop by the teaspoonful 1 inch apart on a buttered and floured baking sheet and bake at 350 degrees for 15 minutes or until brown. Yield: approximately 1½ dozen.

SHOPPING LIST

¾ lb. crab meat
2 bunches watercress
1 head endive
6 shallots
4 lbs. selected fruit

1 lb. shredded coconut
1 pt. light cream
Kirsch
Madeira wine

STAPLES

sugar
eggs
flour
vegetable oil
Dijon mustard
tarragon vinegar

butter

salt
pepper
vanilla extract

Pâté Maison

Ratatouille

Quick Home-Baked Bread

Pears Stuffed with Gorgonzola Cheese

TO SERVE 8

WINE
*A dry Sémillon or one of the
varietal Australian wines.*

REMARKS

IF YOU know any pâté addicts, this unusual little supper will be well received by them. It is a very popular meal in my cooking classes, and one I share often with friends. My favorite way to serve this supper is to place the food in the center of the table after everyone has been seated, and let people help themselves. It is a lovely meal all year round.

METHOD

EVERY dish must be made some time in advance: the pâté a day before, the ratatouille at least 8 hours before, in order to allow the flavors to develop. In the summer the ratatouille may be served cold, and in the winter hot. Place the bread on a little board and let the guests slice it themselves. Serve tiny gherkins, as they complement the pâté, and plenty of fresh, unsalted butter with the bread. The pears may be served whole, halved, or cut into rounds.

Pâté Maison

IN A skillet over a high flame, brown 1 pound pork loin cut into 1-inch chunks in a tablespoon of clarified butter (see Basic Recipe, page 159). Season with ½ teaspoon salt, a pinch of pepper, and ½ teaspoon thyme. Remove the pork and add ¼ pound chicken livers, adding more butter if needed. Brown and season with salt and pepper. Remove the livers, turn off the flame, and add ¼ cup Madeira wine and ¼ cup finely chopped shallots. Scrape up any bits clinging to the skillet. In a large bowl place 1 pound coarsely ground pork and 1 pound finely ground veal. Season with ½ teaspoon salt, a pinch of pepper, thyme, and allspice. Add ¼ cup chopped parsley, 3 table-

8

spoons heavy cream, and 2 eggs. Add the livers and pork chunks, the Madeira, and the shallots. Mix well. Sauté 1 tablespoon of the mixture in order to taste for seasonings. Correct accordingly. Pack into a loaf tin and place in a large pan with water approximately 1 inch deep. Cover the pâté tightly with foil and bake in a 350-degree oven for 2½ hours or until the fat and juices which will have risen to the top are clear yellow. Remove the pâté from the oven and lift off the foil.

Pour off the excess fat and let cool ½ hour. Loosely cover the mold with fresh foil and place a weight on top. (I use a foil-covered brick.) Refrigerate with the weight until chilled. Unmold and slice.

Ratatouille

HEAT ¼ cup olive oil in a large, heavy casserole. Add 2 thinly sliced onions and 2 cloves of garlic, cut in half. (Discard garlic before serving.) When the onions are soft, add 3 green peppers, seeded and quartered; 1 medium eggplant, peeled or not as you wish, sliced ¼ inch thick; 4 zucchini, sliced ¼ inch thick; and 5 tomatoes, sliced ¼ inch thick. Sprinkle salt, pepper, and basil over each layer. Cover and bring to a boil, then cook 2 minutes. Remove cover and reduce liquid, stirring occasionally. Taste for seasoning, correct, and add ½ teaspoon sugar. Cooking time depends upon how well done you like the vegetables. When finished turn off the heat and let the ratatouille stand. Serve hot, at room temperature, or chilled. Garnish with fresh parsley.

Quick Home-Baked Bread

THIS bread may be prepared with the electric mixer.

In a mixing bowl, dissolve 2 packages active dry yeast in ¾ cup warm water. Add 1¼ cups buttermilk, 2½ cups unbleached white flour, ¼ cup lard, 2 tablespoons sugar,

9

2 teaspoons baking powder, and 2 teaspoons salt. Blend 30 seconds on a low speed, scraping the sides and bottom of the bowl. Beat 2 minutes on a medium speed. Stir in 2 to 2½ cups more flour. Dough should remain soft and slightly sticky. Knead about 5 minutes on a generously floured board. Divide the dough into 2 parts, shape into loaves, brush with butter, put in greased loaf pans, and let rise in a warm place until double, about 1 hour. Place on the lowest rack of a 425-degree oven and bake approximately 20 to 25 minutes. Remove from the pan and cool on a wire rack.

Pears Stuffed with Gorgonzola Cheese

PEEL 8 small ripe pears and cut them in half. With a teaspoon, remove the cores and a small amount of the pulp from each half. Cream 3 tablespoons imported Gorgonzola cheese and 3 tablespoons unsalted butter together, until soft and fluffy. Fill the hollows of the pears with the cheese mixture, press the halves together, and roll the

pears in coarsely chopped walnuts until coated. Work quickly to prevent the pears from turning brown. Arrange on a serving plate and chill well.

SHOPPING LIST

1 lb. pork loin
1 lb. ground pork
1 lb. ground veal
¼ lb. chicken livers
4 oz. shallots
3 green peppers
1 medium eggplant
4 zucchini
5 tomatoes
8 small ripe pears

½ pt. heavy cream
2 packages dry yeast
1 qt. buttermilk
small package lard
4 to 6 oz. imported
  Gorgonzola
gherkin pickles
½ lb. walnuts
Madeira wine

STAPLES

eggs
butter
unbleached flour (5 cups)
sugar
olive oil
fresh parsley
garlic
onions (2)

baking powder

salt
pepper
thyme
basil
allspice

Sashimi

Oyako Domburi

Rice

Sliced Sugared Oranges

WINE
Hot sake or Japanese beer.

REMARKS

THIS is an easy and quick Japanese meal. Sashimi is a firm-fleshed, fresh, raw, filleted fish, usually tuna. It is a texture food, having little more than a sweetish bland flavor. It is eaten raw, dipped into a bowl of soy sauce that has been mixed with wasabi powder, a pulverized Japanese green horseradish. The domburi dish is a kind of stew, containing pork, chicken, vegetables, and egg, and is a delicious meal in itself. Ideally, chopsticks should be used for this meal.

METHOD

THE sashimi should be purchased the same day that it is to be used. Keep it well chilled, and shortly before your guests arrive, slice and arrange it attractively on small lacquered trays. Have the soy sauce and wasabi powder mixed and ready. The sashimi makes an ideal hors d'oeuvre served with drinks before dinner. Just before serving, finish preparing the domburi, being certain not to overcook the vegetables. Let the eggs set while everyone is getting settled at the table. Bring it in immediately and serve it from your wok or paella pan. The sugared oranges should be chilled well, waiting in the refrigerator. Japanese fortune cookies are a nice touch at the end of this meal.

Note

JAPANESE cooking and serving utensils are available in Japanese hardware stores, and food ingredients in Japanese markets.

Sashimi

AT A Japanese fish market buy a pound of sashimi,

usually fresh tuna fillet. Just before serving, slice the fish and arrange it on a tray. Serve with Japanese soy sauce mixed with wasabi powder in the following amounts: ¼ cup soy sauce, 1 teaspoon or more wasabi powder. Be cautious: the horseradish is extremely piquant.

Oyako Domburi

CUT the following into bias strips about 1 inch long: 1 bunch of celery, leaves and all, 2 bunches of green onions, and ½ pound mushrooms. Cut 3 onions into 8 pieces each and thinly slice 2 seeded green peppers. Heat 2 tablespoons vegetable oil in a wok, paella pan, or heavy iron skillet. Add all the vegetables and allow them to cook until they begin to soften, tossing constantly with two long-handled wooden spoons, for about 1 minute. Then add 4 tablespoons Mirin wine (Japanese wine) and 1 tablespoon bottled Chinese oyster sauce. Remove from the heat. In another pan, heat 1 teaspoon vegetable oil and add 1 pound pork loin and 2 whole skinned, boned chicken breasts, both cut into thin strips. Cook the chicken and pork only until they change color, about 5 minutes, and then add the meats to the vegetables. This much may be done well ahead. Just before serving cook the whole mixture over a brisk flame, stirring now and then until the vegetables are tender but still crisp, about 1 minute. Then add 6 well-beaten eggs, pouring the eggs over the vegetables and meat in a spiral so as to cover them completely. Do not stir mixture after adding the eggs. Let the eggs set, about 5 minutes, over a low flame and serve immediately.

Rice

USING long-grain rice, follow the directions on the package, substituting chicken stock for water.

Sliced Sugared Oranges

Use approximately 1½ juice oranges per guest. With a sharp paring knife, peel and seed the oranges, being certain also to cut away the white membrane under the peel. Slice the oranges into thin rounds and sprinkle liberally with finely granulated sugar and 2 or 3 tablespoons Grand Marnier. Chill until ready to serve.

SHOPPING LIST

1 lb. sashimi
1 lb. pork loin
2 whole chicken breasts
1 bunch celery
2 bunches green onions
½ lb. mushrooms
2 green peppers

10 juice oranges
small can wasabi powder
Japanese soy sauce
small bottle Chinese
  oyster sauce
Grand Marnier
Mirin wine

STAPLES

eggs (6)
finely granulated sugar
vegetable oil

onions (3)
chicken stock
rice

Stacked Crêpes and Ham

Sliced Herbed Tomatoes

Peaches in Caramel Sauce

TO SERVE 4

WINE
*French Muscadet, California
Sylvaner, or a German May
Wine, in season.*

THIS is an informal, rich little supper that is fun to make for four or six friends on, say, a Sunday evening. Provided all the ingredients, including the crêpes, are at hand, this simple meal may be prepared in about half an hour.

METHOD

ASSEMBLE the stacked crêpes ready for the oven, prepare the tomatoes and allow to marinate. The sauce for the peaches may be prepared with the peaches added but not heated. Fifteen minutes before serving, put the assembled crêpes in the oven. The peaches may be warmed just before serving.

Stacked Crêpes and Ham

MAKE sixteen 5-inch crêpes (see Basic Recipe, page 160), and hold. Prepare 2 cups of cheesed white sauce (see below) and hold. Bring to room temperature 1 pound good-quality boiled ham. Slice the ham into 12 slices approximately the same size as the crêpes. Butter a large flat ovenproof casserole. Place 4 crêpes side by side on the bottom of the dish and cover each crêpe with a slice of ham. Spread some of the cheese sauce (see below) over the ham and then cover with another crêpe. Continue stacking, ending with a crêpe on the top. Spoon a generous amount of sauce over each stack. When nearly ready to serve, place in a 350-degree oven until hot and bubbling, about 10 minutes.

Cheesed White Sauce

IN A heavy saucepan, melt 4 tablespoons butter and blend

17

in 4 tablespoons flour. Stir until smooth and cook for a few minutes. Stirring constantly, blend in 1½ to 2 cups hot milk. Continue to stir until the sauce thickens. Blend in 6 ounces grated imported Gruyère cheese and stir until smooth.

Sliced Herbed Tomatoes

SLICE 3 firm, ripe peeled tomatoes thinly and evenly. Arrange in overlapping slices on a platter. Sprinkle with salt, freshly ground pepper, a pinch of sugar, and lots of minced fresh or dried basil. Drizzle with olive oil and red wine vinegar. Sprinkle with 2 tablespoons minced parsley. Let stand at least 30 minutes.

Peaches in Caramel Sauce

PEEL and halve 4 fresh peaches. In a heavy skillet, melt ¼ pound unsalted butter, add ¾ cup sugar, and melt, stirring constantly with a wire whisk, over a low flame. Add approximately ½ cup Madeira wine, continuing to stir. When the sauce is smooth, add the peach halves. Turn over several times, spooning the syrup over them, allowing them to warm. Serve in a glass dish with plenty of the caramel sauce. Pass a bowl of whipped cream.

To peel peaches

DROP the peaches into rapidly boiling water for 20 seconds. Remove peaches and peel immediately or later, just before using. If they are to stand peeled for more than 5 minutes, put them into a bowl of lemon juice and water so that the outside will not discolor.

SHOPPING LIST

1 lb. boiled ham
6 oz. imported Gruyère
  cheese
3 tomatoes

4 firm ripe peaches
½ pt. heavy cream
Madeira wine

STAPLES

milk
eggs
butter
flour
sugar

olive oil
red wine vinegar
fresh parsley

fresh or dried basil

Hearty Dinners

Potage Bonne Femme

(Cream of Leek and Potato Soup)

Coq au Vin

(Chicken in Red Wine)

Butter Lettuce and Parsley Salad

Petits Pois à la Française

(Peas French Style)

Hazelnut Meringue Cake

TO SERVE 8

WINE
The wine you cook with. This is one meal for which you do not serve white wine with fowl. For dessert, Angelica or a tawny Port.

REMARKS

THIS is a French meal that includes both a classic soup and a classic chicken dish. Cream of leek and potato soup is a soup in its own right as well as a base for many other French soups. Chicken cooked in red wine is a dish that every serious cook should know how to make. The hazelnut meringue cake is my favorite cake in the book.

METHOD

BAKE the cake in advance, keeping the filling separate and refrigerated. Assemble the cake an hour or so before your guests arrive. Everything else may be made well ahead, and reheated before serving. Be careful not to overcook the chicken as you reheat it. A butter lettuce and parsley salad may be served after the chicken.

Potage Bonne Femme
(Cream of Leek and Potato Soup)

MELT 2 tablespoons butter in a soup pot. Add 4 medium potatoes, finely sliced, and the white parts of 6 leeks, washed thoroughly and shredded. Reserve the green of one leek for garnishing. Season with salt and cayenne pepper and stir over a slow fire until the vegetables are softened. Add 4 cups milk and stir over a medium fire until it comes to a boil. Simmer, covered, for 20 minutes. Put the mixture through a sieve or a food mill. Return the soup to the pot, add 3 egg yolks beaten with 1 cup heavy cream, and thicken over a slow fire, stirring constantly. When ready to serve, reheat and add more cream if it is too thick. Garnish each bowl with the finely shredded green of the leek.

Coq au Vin
(Chicken in Red Wine)

BLANCH 4 slices of bacon cut into pieces with 24 tiny peeled* white onions in boiling water for 30 seconds. Drain well. Brown a cut-up 4-pound capon in 2 tablespoons butter, remove, and then brown the bacon and onions in the same pot. Return the chicken to the pot, pour ½ cup warmed brandy over the chicken, and flame. Add enough good-quality red burgundy wine to come about ¼ of the way up the sides of the pot. Add a clove of crushed garlic and a bouquet garni (see page 158). Cover and cook in the oven at 350 degrees or on top of the stove for about 40 minutes or until done. When the chicken is tender, remove to a serving dish to keep warm, remove the bouquet garni from the liquid, and thicken the wine sauce slightly with a beurre manié (see page 158), starting with a piece the size of a pea and adding more if needed. The sauce should be thin, thickened just enough to barely cling to the chicken. Adjust the seasoning. Sprinkle with chopped parsley when ready to serve.

*Be sure not to cut off root end of onion.

Petits Pois à la Française
(Peas French Style)

PUT 2 tablespoons butter in a saucepan and add 8 leaves of butter lettuce, shredded, ½ teaspoon salt, 1½ teaspoons sugar, 1 tablespoon chopped parsley, and ½ teaspoon chervil. Add 2 generous cups freshly shelled peas, mix all together, and finish cooking until barely tender, using the Paul Mayer Method (page 159), adding not more than ½ cup boiling water. There should only be a tablespoon or so of water left in the pot. If desired, a small piece of beurre manié (see page 158) may be added. Return the pan to the fire, shaking it to roll the peas around until the butter-flour mixture has combined with the liquid.

25

Salad

A butter lettuce and parsley salad (see Basic Recipes on page 162).

Hazelnut Meringue Cake

WHISK 4 egg whites until stiff, then beat in gradually, 1 tablespoon at a time, a cup of finely granulated sugar. Continue beating until very stiff, adding 1 teaspoon vanilla and ½ teaspoon vinegar. Last, fold in 5 ounces toasted (in the oven for 5 minutes at 350 degrees), ground hazelnuts (8 ounces of nuts with shells are roughly 5 ounces shelled). Pour into two 8-inch greased and floured cake tins and bake 30 to 40 minutes in a 375-degree oven, until delicately browned.

Apricot Cream Filling

SOAK 4 ounces dried apricots overnight in a little water, add 4 tablespoons sugar and the juice from half a lemon; cover, and simmer gently until soft enough to sieve. Whip 1 cup heavy cream with 2 tablespoons powdered sugar. Carefully fold in the sieved or puréed apricots. Spread the apricot-flavored cream generously on the bottom layer of the cake. Add the top layer and sprinkle with powdered sugar. Any additional apricot cream may be served on the side.

Note

IF hazelnuts are not available, substitute browned, ground walnuts. Nuts may be ground quickly in the blender or nut grinder and spread on a metal tray to brown in the oven.

SHOPPING LIST

4-lb. capon
6 leeks
24 tiny white onions
small head butter lettuce
2 lbs. fresh green peas
½ lb. hazelnuts

4 oz. package dried
  apricots
1 pt. heavy cream
good-quality red
  burgundy wine
brandy

STAPLES

potatoes (4)
milk (1 qt.)
eggs (6)
bacon
garlic
flour
parsley
butter
sugar, granulated and
  powdered

white vinegar
lemon

salt
cayenne pepper
bouquet garni
chervil
vanilla extract

Velouté de Tomates à la Provençale

(Tomato Soup Country Style)

Navarin des Quatre Saisons

(Braised Lamb and Potatoes)

Romaine Salad

Pear and Banana Tart

WINE
*Serve the same wine you cook
with or a Sauvignon Blanc,
or, from France, a
Montrachet.*

TO SERVE 8

THIS is a hearty French provincial-style meal, with an unusual tomato soup that is thickened with rice. The lamb is highly seasoned with garlic, and the pear and banana tart is my own combination. This is an easy dinner to prepare and serve.

FINISH preparing the soup in advance and reheat before serving. The lamb and potatoes can be finished ahead and kept warm. The tart may be prepared ahead but not baked until the guests arrive so that you may serve it warm. I use a paella pan to cook the potatoes, and present the dish at the table in the paella pan, lamb over the potatoes, garnished with parsley.

Velouté de Tomates à la Provençale
(Tomato Soup Country Style)

SAUTÉ 10 minced slices of bacon in a heavy skillet. Discard all but 2 tablespoons of fat and add 2 chopped onions and 2 chopped leeks, white parts only. Sauté gently for about 5 minutes. Peel and seed 2½ pounds ripe tomatoes and mash into the pan with the bacon, onions, and leeks. Sauté for 10 minutes more. Add ½ cup light sauterne wine and 1½ cups chicken stock. Discard the tough outer leaves of a small young cabbage and finely mince the heart. Add to the tomato mixture. Season with salt and pepper, 1½ teaspoons dried basil, 1 teaspoon dried thyme, and 1 teaspoon sugar. Simmer gently, uncovered, for 40 minutes. Meanwhile, cook ⅓ cup rice until it is soft and mushy. Combine, batch by batch in an electric blender, the soup, rice, and 2 peeled cloves of garlic. (Garlic is optional.)

Purée briefly so that the soup does not become too smooth. Return the soup to the pot, add ½ cup more sauterne and ½ cup water and simmer gently, covered, for 30 minutes. Adjust seasoning. If it is not thick enough, simmer uncovered until it reduces to the right consistency. Serve very hot.

Navarin
(Braised Lamb)

HEAT 4 tablespoons clarified butter (see page 159) in a heavy casserole and quickly brown 4 pounds cubed lamb over a high flame. Pour off the excess fat and add 3 or more cloves of crushed garlic, 2 tablespoons flour, 1 teaspoon thyme, 1 bay leaf, 4 tablespoons chopped parsley, 1½ cups dry white wine, and ½ cup chicken stock. Season with salt and white pepper and cook covered over a moderate heat for 20 minutes or to the desired degree of doneness. Remove the meat to be kept warm, and reduce the liquid. Check the seasoning and, if desired, strain the sauce.

Potatoes

MELT 4 tablespoons butter in a large open casserole or paella pan. Add 2½ pounds peeled potatoes cut into small pieces, sprinkle with salt, white pepper, and enough chicken stock to just cover the potatoes. Place in a 425-degree oven and bake until the stock is cooked away. Serve the lamb over the potatoes, pour the sauce over the lamb, and garnish each plate with minced parsley.

Salad

SEE romaine salad in the Basic Recipes (page 162).

Pear and Banana Tart

PREPARE a tart pastry (see Basic Recipe, page 163), chill, and roll out to about ⅛ inch thickness. Shape into an 8-inch tart tin. Dot the pastry with bits of unsalted butter, sprinkle with sugar, and add 1 layer each of thinly sliced, peeled pears and bananas. Sprinkle each new layer with sugar and dot with butter. Place the tart on the floor of a 425-degree preheated gas oven for 10 minutes or over the coils on top of an electric stove for 7 minutes, in order to brown the lower crust. Finish baking on the rack of a 350-degree oven for about 10 minutes more, or until the crust is nicely browned.

SHOPPING LIST

1 lb. bacon
4 lbs. cut-up lamb, shoulder or leg
2½ lbs. ripe tomatoes
1 small white cabbage
2 leeks

4 ripe pears
4 ripe bananas
2 heads romaine lettuce
light sauterne wine
dry white wine

STAPLES

eggs
butter (½ lb.)
flour
sugar
vegetable oil
parsley
garlic
onions
potatoes (2½ lbs.)
chicken stock (4 cups)

rice
red wine vinegar

salt
pepper
thyme
basil
bay leaf
white pepper

31

Cold Cream of Cucumber Soup

Veal Ragout

Fettuccine with Butter and Parsley

Lemon Cake

TO SERVE 8

WINE
With the soup, an Italian
Verdicchio or a California
Pinot Blanc; for the veal
Valpolicella from Italy or a
California Zinfandel.

THIS is a good summer menu and one that has been my favorite meal to travel with. The lemon cake is a popular one; when served partially frozen, it has a texture similar to cheesecake. This menu can quite easily be adapted to serve 12 or 14 people at a buffet.

Travel Method

FINISH the cucumber soup the day before and chill in a covered plastic container. The lemon cake should be baked and frozen the day before as well. In the morning brown and completely assemble the veal ragout so that it can be put into the oven whenever you are ready. The soup and cake go into the ice chest and hours later arrive still chilled.

Regular Method

HAVE the cucumber soup well chilled and on the table when your guests sit down. Forty minutes before serving, put the room-temperature veal into a preheated oven, being careful not to overcook it. The pasta holds nicely on top of the stove, ready to be tossed with butter and parsley just before serving.

Cold Cream of Cucumber Soup

PEEL, cut in half lengthwise, scoop out the seeds, and slice 4 large cucumbers. Cook in 2 tablespoons butter over low heat about 10 minutes. Stir in 3 tablespoons flour and gradually add 2 cups chicken stock, stirring constantly. Add 1 cup of milk scalded with 4 thin slices of onion. Simmer slowly for 15 minutes. Put the soup in the blender and purée. Stir in ½ to 1 cup heavy cream, depending upon the thickness of the soup, season with salt and white pepper, and chill. This soup is lovely served in glass bowls and garnished with a thin slice of scored cucumber.

Veal Ragout

CUT 2½ pounds veal shoulder into small cubes. Brown the meat quickly in hot clarified butter (see page 159) in a heavy pan. Remove the meat and add 1 finely chopped large onion. Cook slowly, until the onion is lightly browned. Return the meat to the pan and add 2 tablespoons sweet paprika, 2 teaspoons salt, ½ teaspoon sugar, 2 large tomatoes cut into 8 pieces each, 2 medium-sized green peppers, seeded and cut into small pieces, and 1 tablespoon caraway seeds (optional). About 40 minutes before serving, cover and place in a preheated 375-degree oven. Stir occasionally to prevent scorching.

Fettuccine with Butter and Parsley

COOK 1 pound fettuccine in lots of boiling, salted water until barely tender. Drain, return to the pot, and toss with ¼ pound unsalted butter and 3 tablespoons fresh, minced parsley. Add salt and white pepper to taste. Keep warm or reheat and serve with the veal.

Lemon Cake

LIGHTLY butter a 7-inch springform pan. Line the bottom and sides of the pan with ladyfingers. Blend thoroughly 1 can sweetened, condensed milk with 4 egg yolks, 1 teaspoon freshly grated lemon rind, and the juice of 3 large or 4 small lemons. Beat the 4 egg whites with ½ teaspoon cream of tartar until stiff, and fold into the lemon mixture. Pour the batter into the pan and bake in a 375-degree oven until the top is nicely browned, about 20 to 30 minutes. Put into the freezer until ready to serve.

SHOPPING LIST

2½ lbs. veal shoulder
4 cucumbers
2 large tomatoes
2 green peppers
1 lb. (fresh if possible) fettuccine

1 doz. ladyfingers
1 can sweetened condensed milk
½ pt. heavy cream

STAPLES

milk
eggs (4)
butter
flour
fresh parsley
onions (2)
lemons (4)

chicken stock

salt
pepper
sweet Hungarian paprika
cream of tartar
caraway seeds (optional)

Ceviche

Paella Valenciana

Garlic Toast

Romaine Salad

Strawberries with Cream

TO SERVE 8

WINE
*California Barbera or a
Spanish Rioja—for dessert,
Lagrima from Málaga or a
California Gold Muscatel.*

REMARKS

THIS is a menu containing two classically Spanish dishes you might be served in any part of Spain. Ceviche, always made with a firm-fleshed regional white fish, is a marinated raw fish salad. The lime juice marinates and "cooks" the fish. The distinguishing ingredients of paella are saffron, rice, chicken, and shellfish—the shellfish varying greatly according to the region. A paella pan is an important part of the presentation and one should be used. Since the paella contains shellfish, poultry, meat, rice, and vegetables, no side dishes are needed.

METHOD

THE ceviche should marinate 5 or 6 hours before serving and makes a good hors d'oeuvre with cocktails. Finish the paella to the point of its last baking, putting it into the oven 25 minutes before serving, adding the seafood the last 4 or 5 minutes. Don't overcook it as the paella tends to get dry. Crisp garlic toast is a nice accompaniment to the paella with a romaine salad following. Berries for dessert make a simple end to this meal. The paella in its pan is such a beautiful dish it should always be served at the table.

Ceviche

CUT 1 pound of a boned and skinned firm white fish, such as halibut, into small pieces. Put them into a deep china, pottery, or glass dish. Add half a small onion finely chopped, 3 tablespoons finely chopped cilantro (Chinese parsley), and chopped green chilies to taste. Pour ¾ cup fresh lime juice and 2 tablespoons olive oil over the mixture and let marinate at least 4 or 5 hours in the refrigerator.

37

Paella Valenciana

In a paella pan sauté a cut-up 3-pound chicken in ½ cup foaming butter to which 2 cloves of crushed garlic have been added. When the chicken is golden brown, remove and set aside. In the juices remaining sauté 2 cups rice until golden. Add ¼ teaspoon saffron, or more to taste, and 4 cups chicken stock and bring the liquid to a boil. Season with salt and pepper. Cook the rice uncovered over a low flame for 20 minutes. Now add the chicken pieces with 2 or 3 sliced Chorizo sausage (or any spiced sausage) and ¾ cup diced pimientos. With a large cooking spoon mix the chicken, rice, sausage, and pimiento together. This much may be prepared well ahead. When ready, bake in a preheated 350-degree oven uncovered for approximately 20 to 25 minutes. Add more chicken stock if needed. Add large shelled shrimp, clams, and mussels in their shells, and shelled lobster tails and cook until the clams open and the shellfish is red, about 4 or 5 minutes more. Serve from the paella pan and be sure that each guest gets some of everything in the dish.

Garlic Toast

Soften 4 ounces unsalted butter and blend thoroughly with 2 crushed cloves of garlic. Cut a loaf of French bread in half lengthwise. Cover generously with the garlic-butter and put into a 400-degree oven for 7 or 8 minutes, until golden and crisp. Slice and serve immediately.

Romaine Salad

See Basic Recipes, page 162.

Strawberries with Cream

In a saucepan combine ¼ cup sugar and ¼ cup water.

Bring the mixture to a boil, and simmer 5 minutes. Add 2 tablespoons Kirsch and pour over 3 pints cleaned and hulled ripe strawberries. Chill. Serve with whipped cream that has been sweetened with powdered sugar and flavored with a few drops of vanilla extract.

SHOPPING LIST

1 lb. firm white fish
  fillet (halibut, red
  snapper, etc.)
2 dozen clams
2 dozen mussels
2 fresh lobster tails
3-lb. chicken
2 or 3 Chorizo or other
  highly spiced sausages
1 bunch cilantro
  (Chinese parsley)

7 limes
2 heads romaine lettuce
3 pts. ripe strawberries
  small can chopped
    Mexican green chilies
3 small cans pimientos
½ pt. heavy cream
loaf of French bread
Kirsch

STAPLES

butter
sugar
olive oil
vegetable oil
garlic
onions
chicken stock (4 cups)

rice (2 cups)
red wine vinegar
vanilla extract

salt
pepper
saffron

Marinated Sweet Peppers

Ground Meat Loaf with Tomato Sauce

Purée de Pommes de Terre aux Fines Herbes
(Puréed Herbed Potatoes)

Pots de Crème à la Vanille
(Individual Vanilla Custards)

TO SERVE 6

WINE
Grenache or Gamay Rosé

Whenever I announce this menu to my classes, a few people say they need not come to me to learn how to prepare meat loaf and mashed potatoes. On the other hand, there are those who enjoy cooking a family dinner, and I count it as one of my favorites. It makes a perfect Sunday afternoon meal, when families with children often get together. The cold meat loaf makes delicious sandwiches.

METHOD

The pots de crème may be prepared in the morning and placed in the refrigerator to chill. The peppers should marinate 2 or 3 hours and are delicious served with cocktails before dinner. The meat loaf may be finished baking a half hour before serving and allowed to rest in a warm place until ready to slice. The mashed potatoes wait very nicely in their pot on top of the stove for reheating or, if they are to be served for a buffet, can be kept in a covered serving dish in a warm oven.

Marinated Sweet Peppers

Char 8 sweet green (and red, if possible) peppers over an open flame and remove the skin. Cut into strips and marinate in the vinegar and oil dressing on page 163, adding 2 whole cloves of garlic and 1 tablespoon or more of minced parsley to the marinade. Discard the garlic before serving.

Ground Meat Loaf with Tomato Sauce

Place 1 pound ground beef, ½ pound ground veal, and ½ pound ground pork in a large bowl. In the electric

41

blender place 4 slices white bread that have been soaked in milk and then squeezed dry. Add salt, black pepper, an onion cut into pieces, 2 tablespoons tomato purée, and 3 to 5 tablespoons mayonnaise, depending upon how moist you prefer the loaf. Run the blender on low speed until everything is chopped and well mixed. Add the ingredients to the meat in the bowl, and mix thoroughly with your hands. Correct the seasoning, pack the loaf into a well-greased loaf pan, and bake 60 minutes in a preheated 375-degree oven. When it is done remove the loaf from the oven, pour off any accumulated fat, and allow it to rest at least 20 minutes before slicing. Serve with tomato sauce, page 164.

Purée de Pommes de Terre aux Fines Herbes
(Puréed Herbed Potatoes)

BOIL 2 pounds peeled, quartered potatoes until soft but not mushy. Drain and put through a sieve or food mill and return the purée to the pan. Add salt and pepper to taste, 4 or more tablespoons unsalted butter, and gradually stir in enough light cream to obtain the desired consistency, blending over a very low flame. Add all or any combination of the following herbs: chopped parsley, chives, chervil, tarragon. Start by adding a teaspoon, tasting, and adding more if desired.

Pots de Crème à la Vanille
(Individual Vanilla Custards)

SCALD 2 cups heavy cream with 2 teaspoons vanilla and ½ cup sugar. Remove from heat and add 6 beaten egg yolks, stirring constantly. Strain the mixture through a fine sieve into small custard pots. Set the pots in a pan of water, cover, and bake in a 325-degree oven for about 15 minutes, or until done. Serve well chilled.

SHOPPING LIST

1 lb. ground lean beef
½ lb. ground pork loin
½ lb. ground veal
8 sweet peppers
sliced white bread
1 can tomato purée

1 large can Italian-type
   tomatoes
1 small can tomato paste
1 pt. heavy cream
1 pt. light cream
fresh chives (optional)

STAPLES

milk
butter
sugar
olive oil
fresh parsley
onions
potatoes (2 lbs.)
mayonnaise
lemons

red wine vinegar

salt
pepper
chervil
tarragon
basil
vanilla extract

Zuppa di Vongole

(Fresh Clam Soup)

Lingua di Bue Brasata

(Beef Tongue Braised in Red Wine)

Pommes de Terre Mont Rouge

(Potato-Carrot Purée)

Granite

(Fruit-Flavored Ices)

TO SERVE 8

WINE
Unless you use a superb wine to braise with, drink a different one—a robust California Cabernet Sauvignon or any Beaujolais Red.

REMARKS

IT HAS been my experience that many Americans have never tasted tongue. Beef tongue is a tender, succulent, tasty meat, and an economical cut besides. The shape is what most people object to, and once the tongue is sliced, the original shape is hard to imagine. After all the protest in my classes over cooking and eating tongue, everyone agreed it was absolutely delicious after eating it. Any cut of beef pot roast may be substituted for the tongue on this menu; simply eliminate the preboiling step. I always serve the delicious clam soup in large white soup bowls. The red soup and the white bowls make a striking combination.

METHOD

EVERYTHING must be prepared well in advance. Begin the ices at least 6 hours ahead of time. The tongue may be removed from the pot when done, sliced, placed on a serving platter, covered lightly, and kept warm. Finish preparing the sauce and reheat it before serving. Finish the potatoes and reheat them. Prepare the soup just before your guests arrive, leaving the tomato sauce and clams separate. Reheat the tomato sauce before pouring it over the steamed clams.

Zuppa di Vongole
(Fresh Clam Soup)

HEAT 6 tablespoons olive oil in a heavy deep saucepan. Add 2 crushed cloves of garlic and cook, stirring over a moderate heat for about 30 seconds. Pour in 1 cup dry white wine, add 5 pounds ripe tomatoes that have been peeled, seeded, and coarsely chopped, and bring to a boil.

45

Reduce the heat and simmer the sauce, partially covered, for 10 minutes. Scrub 2 to 4 dozen clams, depending upon how many clams you wish to serve each guest, and drop them into a heavy skillet containing about ⅛ inch of boiling bottled clam juice or water. Cover tightly and steam the clams over a high heat for 5 minutes, until they open. Strain all the clam juice in the skillet through a cloth into the simmering tomato sauce. The soup can wait at this point. Just before serving, transfer the clams to large heated soup plates and reheat the tomato sauce for a minute or two. Pour it over the clams, and sprinkle with chopped parsley.

Lingua di Bue Brasata
(Beef Tongue Braised in Red Wine)

In a large pot, cover a 4-pound fresh beef tongue with cold water. Add an onion stuck with cloves, bring to a boil, cover, reduce the heat, and simmer for 2 hours. Remove the tongue from the pot and reserve the liquid. When the tongue is cool enough, remove the skin and cut away the fat, bones, and gristle at its base. Preheat the oven to 350 degrees. In a heavy flameproof casserole heat 1 tablespoon olive oil and brown the tongue on both sides. Remove the tongue and add 1 cup finely chopped onions, ½ cup finely chopped carrots, and ½ cup finely chopped, peeled celery. Cook the vegetables over moderate heat, stirring frequently, until they are softened and lightly browned. Pour in ¾ cup dry red wine and boil briskly for a minute. Place the tongue on top of the vegetables, add 2 cups of the tongue stock (just barely cover the tongue), ¼ cup chopped parsley, and half a bay leaf. Bring to a simmer, cover, and place in the oven for approximately 1½ hours, or until the tongue is tender. Let the tongue rest 20 minutes and slice thinly. Strain the braising liquid and boil until the sauce thickens slightly, or put the vegetables through a food mill and return them to the liquid

to make a thicker sauce. Reheat the sauce when ready
to serve and spoon over the tongue slices.

Pommes de Terre Mont Rouge
(Potato-Carrot Purée)

Cook separately in boiling salted water 6 potatoes and
8 medium-sized carrots. Drain the vegetables and put them
through a fine sieve. Beat into the combined carrots and
potatoes 1 to 2 cups light cream, 1 egg yolk, and ¼ pound
unsalted butter. Season with 1 teaspoon Dijon mustard,
salt, and white pepper to taste.

Granite
(Fruit-Flavored Ices)

The following amounts make about 1½ pints of each
flavor.

Lemon Ice	*Orange Ice*	*Strawberry Ice*
2 cups water	2 cups water	1 cup water
1 cup sugar	¾ cup sugar	½ cup sugar
1 cup fresh lemon juice	1 cup fresh orange juice	2 cups puréed fresh berries
	juice of 1 lemon	2 tablespoons fresh lemon juice

In a 2-quart saucepan, bring the water and sugar to a
boil over moderate heat. Timing from the moment the
sugar and water begin to boil, let the mixture keep boiling
for exactly 5 minutes. Immediately remove the pan from
the heat and let the syrup cool. Stir in the fruit juices
or purée. Pour the mixture into a shallow dish or pie pan
and freeze. Stir with a fork every 30 minutes or so, scraping
into the mixture the ice particles that form around the
edges. The finished ice should have a fine, snowy texture.
Serve in champagne glasses.

SHOPPING LIST

4 lbs. fresh beef tongue
2 to 4 dozen fresh clams
8 medium-sized carrots
5 lbs. tomatoes
1 bunch celery
1 small can clam nectar
1 pint light cream

dry white wine
dry red wine

For Ices
5 lemons
7 oranges
2 pts. strawberries

STAPLES

olive oil
garlic
parsley
onions
butter
eggs
sugar

potatoes (6)

cloves
bay leaf
Dijon mustard
salt
white pepper

Eilene's Portuguese Seafood Stew

Rice with Peas

Garlic Toast

Butter Lettuce and Parsley Salad with Cheeses

Rich Chocolate Cake

TO SERVE 8

WINE
*Either Portuguese Vinho
Verde or California Pinot
Chardonnay*

REMARKS

My friend Eilene brought this sensational recipe back from a recent visit to her family in Portugal. I have gotten nothing but raves from the people in my classes for this dish. The quick and easy cake is the chocolate cake most preferred by my children and friends. This meal is deliciously filling and informal and one of my favorites.

METHOD

THE stew without the fish should be made in the morning and left all day to increase the flavors. Four or five minutes before serving, add the fish and shrimp and reheat, being careful not to overcook the seafood. Gently reheat the rice and peas and turn into attractive serving dishes. Serve at the table in large white soup bowls, if you have them. Place the fish on top of the rice and serve plenty of garlic toast. A separate butter lettuce salad course, served at the table with one or two cheeses, is suggested.

Eilene's Portuguese Seafood Stew

IN A large deep pot heat 1 tablespoon olive oil and 1 tablespoon butter. Add 1 large, chopped onion, and a clove of minced garlic. When the onion is softened, add 1 large green pepper, seeded and chopped, 1 large carrot, chopped, and 4 medium tomatoes, peeled and chopped. Stir together and add 1 cup beef stock, ½ cup dry white wine, ½ teaspoon sugar, 1 teaspoon or more of fresh or dried chopped basil, ½ teaspoon or more of paprika, and salt and pepper to taste. Bring the mixture to a boil, then reduce the heat and simmer for 15 minutes. Just before serving, add 2 pounds cubed red snapper fillets (or any firm white fish fillets) and simmer about 2 minutes. Then add 1 pound

50

shelled and deveined raw shrimp and cook until they turn pink—about 30 seconds. Garnish each serving with chopped parsley and serve in large soup bowls over rice with peas.

Rice with Peas

BRING to a boil 3⅓ cups chicken stock and water. Add 1½ cups long-grain rice and cook about 15 minutes. Then add approximately 2 cups fresh peas, 3 tablespoons butter, and salt to taste, and cook until the rice and peas are done, about 10 minutes more.

Garlic Toast

SOFTEN 4 ounces unsalted butter and blend thoroughly with 2 crushed cloves of garlic. Cut a loaf of French bread in half lengthwise. Cover generously with the garlic butter and put into a 400-degree oven for 7 or 8 minutes, until golden and crisp. Slice and serve immediately.

Butter Lettuce and Parsley Salad

SEE Basic Recipes, page 162.

Rich Chocolate Cake

IF possible, make this cake in an electric mixer. In a large mixing bowl combine 1⅔ cups flour, 1½ cups sugar, 1 cup unsweetened cocoa, 1½ teaspoons baking soda, 1 teaspoon salt, 4 ounces unsalted butter, 1½ cups buttermilk, 1 teaspoon vanilla, and 2 eggs. Blend on a low speed 30 seconds, scraping sides and bottom of the bowl. Beat 3 minutes on medium speed. Pour into two 8-inch layer pans that have been greased and floured. Bake in a preheated 350-degree oven 30 to 35 minutes, or until done. When finished baking, turn out onto racks to cool. Frost between layers and on top as desired (see below).

Icing

IN A heavy saucepan, melt 6 tablespoons unsalted butter, add 3 ounces semisweet chocolate and melt, stirring constantly. Add 1¼ cups light brown sugar and ¾ cup heavy cream. Bring to a boil, and boil about 3 minutes, or until thick enough to spread. Cool slightly before spreading.

SHOPPING LIST

2 lbs. red snapper or any other firm white fish fillets
1 lb. raw shrimp
1 bunch carrots
1 large green pepper
4 ripe tomatoes
2 lbs. fresh peas
2 heads butter lettuce

several salad cheeses
1 quart buttermilk
small can unsweetened cocoa
3 ounces semisweet chocolate
½ pt. heavy cream
1 loaf French bread
dry white wine

STAPLES

olive oil
butter
onions
garlic
beef stock (1 cup)
chicken stock (3½ cups)
sugar
light brown sugar
parsley
rice (1½ cups)
vegetable oil

wine vinegar
flour
baking soda
eggs

fresh or dried basil
paprika
salt
pepper
vanilla extract

Swiss Fondue

Entrecôte, Shallot Sauce

Potatoes in Cream

Salad

Lemon Tart

WINE
*A first-quality Bordeaux Red
or California Cabernet
Sauvignon*

TO SERVE 8

REMARKS

NEARLY everyone likes steak, so when I invite finicky eaters for dinner, this is my safe menu. The fondue makes a wonderful hors d'oeuvre or first course. It is enjoyable for your guests to watch it being made as well as fun to eat. The entrecôte, with its shallot sauce, is an interesting way to serve steak, and the lemon tart is rich and light at the same time.

METHOD

PREPARE the fondue either in the living room to be served as an hors d'oeuvre or at the dining table for the first course. Be sure to have all the ingredients at hand when you are making it. Time the potatoes to be done when you are ready to eat. Grill the steaks and finish preparing the shallot sauce ahead of time. When ready to serve, reheat the sauce and coat the steaks. The lemon tart may be served at room temperature or chilled. A romaine salad is recommended.

Swiss Fondue

RUB the inside of an earthenware casserole with a clove of garlic, then discard garlic. Place the casserole over a fondue burner or a chafing-dish rack. Add 1 cup dry white wine and heat. Add 1 pound grated imported* Swiss cheese. Heat the mixture, stirring constantly until the cheese is melted and well blended with the wine. Add 1 teaspoon or more Dijon mustard and 2 tablespoons flour mixed to a paste with a little water. Stir in 2 tablespoons Kirsch. This dish is eaten directly from the casserole, which

*Do not use domestic Swiss cheese as it will curdle.

54

should be kept warm over a low flame. Should the fondue thicken too much, stir in a little more Kirsch. The guests spear torn pieces of French bread with their forks and dip them into the fondue.

Entrecôte, Shallot Sauce

SELECT 8 thin (½-inch-thick) rib eye steaks. Sprinkle with salt and pepper and fry quickly in a little butter in a heavy skillet over high heat to the desired degree of doneness (one-half minute each side for rare). Remove from the pan to a serving platter. Over medium heat, add 4 tablespoons butter to the pan juices, and sauté 12 finely minced shallots, 4 tablespoons or more finely minced parsley, and 1 table-spoon or more dried oregano. Continue cooking gently over the heat until most of the liquid has cooked away. When ready to serve, coat each steak thickly with the resulting sauce.

Potatoes in Cream

PEEL 4 large potatoes and slice them in rounds about ¼ inch thick. Put the slices in a heavy skillet, season with nutmeg, a pinch of salt, and lots of freshly ground pepper. Pour in a cup of milk and simmer uncovered for 15 minutes, turning the potatoes often. Rub the inside of an earthenware casserole with butter, and put the potatoes in. Pour in a cup of heavy cream, dot the top with butter, cover, and place in a 300-degree oven for about 2 hours, or until the cream is absorbed and the potatoes are soft. Check the seasoning and brown the surface under the broiler. Serve hot.

Salad

A ROMAINE salad (Basic Recipes, page 162).

Lemon Tart

MAKE the tart pastry on page 163, chill, roll out to ⅛-inch thickness, and line an 8-inch buttered tart pan with a removable bottom. Grate the outer yellow peel (avoid the white) of 2 large fresh lemons. Put 2 eggs and 3 yolks in a mixing bowl. With a wire whisk, beat in ½ cup confectioners' sugar until smooth. Beat in the juice from the 2 lemons, the grated rind, 2 teaspoons arrowroot that has been blended with 2 tablespoons milk, and 6 table-spoons melted butter. Fill the tart shell, and place the tart on the floor of a 425-degree preheated gas oven for 10 minutes, or over the coils on top of an electric stove for 7 minutes, to brown the bottom crust. Finish baking on the rack of a 350-degree oven for 15 minutes more.

SHOPPING LIST

8 ½-inch-thick entrecôtes (market, rib eye, or any favorite steak cut)
12 shallots
1 lb. imported Swiss cheese

1 loaf French bread
½ pint heavy cream
2 bunches romaine lettuce
dry white wine
Kirsch

STAPLES

garlic
milk
butter
parsley
potatoes (4 large)
flour
eggs
granulated sugar
powdered sugar

lemons (2 large)
arrowroot
vegetable oil
red wine vinegar

Dijon mustard
salt
pepper
fresh or dried oregano

Lamb Curry

Rice with Peas and Onions

Yoghurt Salad

Romaine Lettuce Salad

Mango and Pistachio Mousse

TO SERVE 8

WINE
*Offer beer for those who like
it with curry, or a Chianti
from Italy or California.
With dessert, a California
Moscato Amabile.*

REMARKS

ONE of the menu requests that I get repeatedly from students is for curry. Every cook should know how to prepare at least one good curry. Also, from the cook's point of view, curry is a very easy meal to prepare and serve, and one that is ideal for a large buffet.

METHOD

MAKE the curry well ahead, and reheat when ready to serve. The rice waits very nicely to be reheated slowly. Have all the condiments on the table before the guests sit down. For a condiment server, I use small individual porcelain custard cups on a natural straw tray. It looks pretty and works perfectly. The yoghurt salad is served with the curry, on a small separate plate. I add hot dry mustard to the oil and vinegar dressing for the romaine salad. The mango and pistachio mousse is a delicate and unusual end to this exotic meal.

Lamb Curry

BROWN 3½ pounds cubed lamb, shoulder or leg, in 2 tablespoons clarified butter (see page 159). Remove the meat, lower the flame, and add 3 medium onions, coarsely chopped, 2 peeled stalks of coarsely chopped celery, a coarsely chopped green pepper, and 2 crushed cloves of garlic. Cook the vegetables until they are soft. In a small bowl mix together 4 tablespoons curry powder, 1 teaspoon each of ginger and turmeric, and ½ teaspoon each of paprika, ground cardamom, ground coriander, and cayenne pepper, 2 tablespoons flour, ½ teaspoon salt, and 2 turns of the pepper grinder. Add half of this mixture to the vegetables and allow to cook for a minute or so.

Add 5 ounces canned coconut juice, 10 ounces chicken stock, and 4 to 6 tablespoons plain yoghurt. Stir until the sauce boils and then taste it. Add more of the mixed spices until the curry is to your liking. Return the meat to the pan and cook, covered, until tender. Serve over the rice with peas and onions and with the following condiments: chutney, crumbled bacon, coarsely chopped onions, chopped peanuts, raisins, and grated coconut.

Rice with Peas and Onions

In 3 tablespoons unsalted butter, sauté a large chopped onion until it is softened. Add 3½ cups chicken stock; bring to a boil and add 1½ cups rice. Cook about 15 minutes, then add 2 to 3 cups fresh green peas. Cook until the peas and rice are done, correct the seasoning, and serve.

Yoghurt Salad

Peel, seed and chop coarsely 3 cucumbers and 3 tomatoes. Add 2 tablespoons coarsely chopped red Bermuda onion and mix with plain yoghurt, one spoonful at a time, until the yoghurt nicely coats the vegetables. Salt and pepper to taste and refrigerate until ready to serve.

Salad

A romaine lettuce salad (see page 162). Add hot, dry mustard to taste to the oil and red wine vinegar dressing on page 163.

Mango and Pistachio Mousse

Peel and slice 3 very ripe mangoes. (A drained 8-ounce can of mangoes may be substituted if the fresh are unavailable.) Purée in the blender and put through a fine sieve to remove the fibers. Return to the blender and add ¼ cup shelled pistachio nuts and blend another few seconds. Add ½ cup melted unsalted butter and blend a moment more. In a large bowl beat together 1 whole egg and 3 egg yolks, add ⅓ cup sugar and continue beating until mixture is thick and creamy. Mix mango and egg mixture together, then carefully fold 1 cup stiffly whipped cream and 3 stiffly whisked egg whites into the mixture. Pour into individual dishes. Chill at least 5 hours.

SHOPPING LIST

3½ lbs. boned lamb, shoulder or leg
½ lb. thinly sliced bacon
1 bunch celery
1 green pepper
2 to 3 lbs. fresh green peas
3 large cucumbers
3 tomatoes
1 Bermuda onion
2 heads romaine lettuce

3 ripe mangoes
5-ounce can coconut juice
1 pint plain yoghurt
8 oz. shelled peanuts
8 oz.-package raisins
8 oz.-package shredded coconut
4 oz. shelled pistachio nuts
½ pt. heavy cream
mango chutney

STAPLES

butter
onions (4)
garlic
flour
chicken stock (5 cups)
rice
eggs
sugar
vegetable oil
red wine vinegar

curry powder
ground ginger
ground turmeric
ground cardamom
ground coriander
cayenne pepper
salt
pepper
paprika
dry hot mustard

Soupe à l'Oseille

(Sorrel Soup)

Boeuf à la Mode Marseillaise

(Pot Roast of Beef Marseilles)

Grilled Tomatoes

Crème Renversée au Caramel

(Caramel Custard)

TO SERVE 8

WINE
*French Châteauneuf-du-Pape
or California Barenblut.
With dessert, a French Haut
Sauterne or a Sweet
Sauvignon Blanc, "Château
type," from California*

REMARKS

THIS is another dinner from the French provinces. The sorrel soup, with its tart lemony flavor, makes a refreshing beginning to the meal. The secret of the unusual pot roast is the use of a dry fruit brandy (do not use a sweet liqueur), to give the meat and sauce a delicate, vaguely fruity touch. Be certain not to use canned olives, but the Greek or Italian type preserved in brine or oil. Hot French bread with butter goes well with this meal.

METHOD

PREPARE the pot roast well ahead and slice it thinly on the diagonal. Reheat and arrange the slices on a platter when ready to serve. Finish making the sauce and have the olives and pork cubes waiting to be added as a garnish. Put the tomatoes on a baking sheet, ready to go into the oven when the soup is served. Finish preparing the soup to the point marked in the recipe, reheating and adding final ingredients just before serving. The custard must be well chilled before it is turned out of the mold.

Soupe à l'Oseille
(Sorrel Soup)

WASH 4 bunches sorrel and remove coarse root ends. In a large heavy soup pot, melt 4 tablespoons unsalted butter. Add the sorrel and toss until all the leaves are well coated and softened. Add 4 peeled and thinly sliced potatoes and 4 cups chicken stock. Bring to a gentle boil and simmer, covered, for about 25 minutes. While cooking, mash the potatoes a bit with a fork to thicken the soup. Season to taste with salt and pepper. This much may be done ahead. Just before serving, reheat the soup and carefully add, stirring constantly, 3 egg yolks beaten with ½ cup heavy cream.

62

Boeuf à la Mode Marseillaise
(Pot Roast of Beef Marseilles)

CUT 12 long larding strips from a pound of salt pork and soak them in 1 cup dry blackberry brandy. Cut the rest of the pork in large dice and fry until crisp. Remove and drain on paper towels. Pour 3 tablespoons of the pork fat into a large heavy casserole. Lard a 4-pound beef sirloin, or any favorite-cut pot roast, with the blackberry-marinated salt pork lardoons, saving the brandy. Sprinkle with coarse salt and cracked black pepper, and brown quickly on all sides in the hot pork fat. Remove the roast; add 2 onions coarsely chopped, 4 carrots coarsely chopped, and 3 or more minced cloves of garlic, and sauté lightly. Place the browned beef on its vegetable bed and add 3 bay leaves, a dozen sprigs of parsley, and 2 to 3 teaspoons of dried thyme. Stir 3 tablespoons tomato paste into the reserved brandy and pour over the beef along with enough beef stock to just cover. Bring to a boil over high heat, and place covered in a 350-degree oven for approximately 2 hours, depending upon how well done you like the meat. Lift out the beef and keep warm. Skim off the fat and boil the vegetables 5 minutes over a high heat to draw out the final juices. Strain the liquid into a smaller pot and continue boiling to reduce and concentrate the flavors. Taste for seasoning. Sauté 8 ounces each of both green and black fresh, whole, unpitted Greek or Italian olives in 2 tablespoons of butter for 2 minutes. Slice the meat diagonally, cover with sauce, and garnish with olives and crisp fried pork cubes.

Grilled Tomatoes

SLICE off the tops of 8 medium-sized firm, ripe tomatoes. Sprinkle with salt, pepper, and a little sugar. Dot each with butter and bake in a 400-degree oven for about 10 minutes.

Crème Renversée au Caramel
(Caramel Custard)

SCALD 1 cup heavy cream and 1 cup milk with a vanilla bean or 1 teaspoon vanilla extract. Beat together 3 eggs, 2 egg yolks, and ½ cup sugar until well blended. Remove the vanilla bean from the hot milk and gradually pour the milk into the egg mixture, stirring constantly. Heat 1 cup sugar in a heavy skillet over moderate heat until it is melted. Gradually add ½ cup water and boil until well blended and brown. Pour the caramel into a ring mold, turning the mold around and around until the entire inside is well coated. When the caramel is set, pour the custard into the mold and set the mold in a pan of hot water. Bake in a moderate oven for about 45 minutes, or until done. Cool and chill. When well chilled, unmold onto a serving dish.

SHOPPING LIST

1 lb. salt pork
4- to 5-lb. beef pot roast, cross rib, sirloin, etc.
4 bunches sorrel
4 carrots

8 medium-sized ripe tomatoes
8 oz. fresh black olives
8 oz. fresh green olives
1 pt. heavy cream
dry blackberry brandy

STAPLES

milk
butter
chicken stock (4 cups)
eggs (8)
onions
garlic
parsley
tomato paste
beef stock

sugar
potatoes (4)

cracked peppercorns
coarse salt
bay leaves
thyme
vanilla bean or
    vanilla extract

Lemon Soup

Moussaka à la Turque

French Bread Toast

Salad with Feta Cheese

Melon in Season

WINE
*Minos (a Cretan wine) or a
California Riesling.*

REMARKS

THIS moussaka is another "meal in one"—meat, vegetables, and eggs. It may be prepared as much as a day in advance, refrigerated, and then baked just before serving. Prepared in a charlotte mold and garnished with parsley, it resembles a Turkish fez when it is turned out. It is easy and impressive to serve. The lemon soup is classically Mideastern and in keeping with the rest of the menu.

METHOD

THE last guest's arrival signals the time to put the room-temperature moussaka into the oven. When it has finished cooking, let it stand in a warm place while you serve the soup. After the soup is finished and the dishes cleared away, turn the moussaka out onto a large platter, garnish with parsley to resemble the tassle on a fez, and surround it with hot tomato sauce. Bring it to the table and serve, cut like a cake, with tomato sauce spooned over each serving. A romaine salad with Greek feta cheese, either in the salad or on the side, is the next course. Sliced melon which has been chilling in the refrigerator for at least 2 hours finishes the meal.

Lemon Soup

ADD ⅓ cup rice slowly to 6 cups boiling chicken stock and cook covered until the rice is very soft. Whisk the yolks of 4 eggs with the juice of 2 large lemons, beating them well. Just before serving add ¾ cup heavy cream to the stock and bring to a boil. Pour a little of the hot broth into the lemon-egg mixture, stirring constantly. Remove the soup from the heat and when it has stopped boiling, stir in the egg-broth mixture. Continue to stir the soup for a few seconds and serve immediately. Garnish with a small piece of lemon peel.

Moussaka à la Turque

PLACE 3 eggplants in boiling water for 20 minutes to soften all sides of the eggplant skin. Cut the eggplants into quarters lengthwise and remove the meat, reserving the skins. Chop the eggplant pulp finely and set aside. In a large, deep pot heat 2 tablespoons butter. Add 2 finely chopped onions and a finely chopped clove of garlic. When the onion is softened, increase the heat and add 2 pounds freshly ground lamb shoulder and brown lightly. Then add the chopped eggplant and 2 peeled, seeded, and chopped tomatoes and continue cooking 5 more minutes. Season with 2 or more tablespoons finely chopped parsley, 1 tablespoon chopped basil, salt, and pepper to taste. Add up to 3 tablespoons flour, stirring until the moisture is nearly all absorbed, then add 2 beaten eggs. Oil the sides and bottom of a charlotte mold and line it with the eggplant skins in such a way that they may be later folded over the filling, purple side out. Fill the prepared mold with the meat-vegetable mixture and fold the skins around it so that they meet at the top if possible. If you are not go-

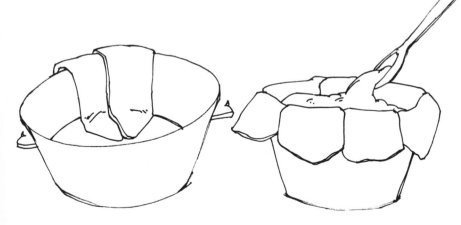

ing to bake the moussaka immediately, put it into the refrigerator until an hour or so before baking. When ready to bake, place the mold in a larger pan of hot water and bake at 375 degrees for 45 minutes, or until firm. Remove from the oven and allow it to stand 20 minutes, then unmold it onto a heated platter. Surround the moussaka with a rich tomato sauce, garnish with parsley, and serve.

Tomato Sauce

See Basic Recipes, page 164.

French Bread Toast

Slice thinly a loaf of French bread and spread each slice generously on both sides with unsalted butter. Place the slices on a cookie sheet and put into a 400-degree oven until lightly toasted.

Salad with Feta Cheese

See Basic Recipes for romaine salad on page 162. Imported Greek feta cheese may be added to the oil and vinegar dressing or may be served on the side. If you serve the cheese, do not salt the dressing.

Melon in Season

Slice and chill a ripe melon for several hours. Serve with a slice of lemon or lime.

SHOPPING LIST

2 lbs. freshly ground
  lamb shoulder
3 medium eggplants
2 large tomatoes
2 heads of romaine
  lettuce
melon in season

½ pt. heavy cream
1 can tomato paste
1 large can Italian
  tomatoes
¼ lb. Greek feta cheese
loaf French bread

STAPLES

lemons (3)
rice
eggs (6)
chicken stock (6 cups)
butter
onions
garlic
parsley

flour
vegetable oil
sugar
red wine vinegar

basil
salt
pepper

More Elegant Dinners

Marinated Broccoli

Poulet Sauté aux Huitres
(Capon with Oysters)

Tomatoes Filled with Green Peas

Mousse au Chocolat

WINE
A Bordeaux such as Côtes de Blaye or a California Grey Riesling.

REMARKS

THIS is an elegant menu, yet one especially easy to serve. The capon is extremely rich and does not call for potatoes, pasta, or rice. A loaf of French bread, which has been warmed in the oven so that the crust is very crisp, is especially nice served with the broccoli. The chocolate mousse is one I learned from Chef Paul Quiaud of Ernie's, and I have not found another to equal it.

METHOD

MAKE the broccoli well ahead of time and have it attractively arranged on individual plates when your guests sit down at the table. The capon, loosely covered and kept warm, waits very nicely for several hours. When you are ready, reheat the sauce, add the oysters, and serve spooned over the capon. The peas in tomato shells add lovely color to the plate.

Marinated Broccoli

WASH and trim 2 bunches of broccoli. Cook according to the Paul Mayer method, page 159, until barely tender. When done, drain and carefully place in a flat serving dish and immediately, while still hot, pour over the following marinade: 8 tablespoons olive oil, 3½ tablespoons freshly squeezed lemon juice, 1 peeled clove of garlic cut in half, 1 tablespoon freshly minced parsley, ½ teaspoon salt, ½ teaspoon pepper.

Allow to marinate 2 hours and serve at room temperature.

Poulet Sauté aux Huitres

(Capon with Oysters)

BROWN a 4-pound cut-up capon in 5 tablespoons unsalted butter, turning the pieces frequently. Then add 1 onion, 2 peeled stalks of celery, ¼ pound mushrooms, and 2 tablespoons parsley, all finely chopped. Cover the pot and continue cooking the chicken in a 350-degree oven for about 40 minutes, or until done. Place the chicken pieces on a serving dish and keep warm. Place the pot over the fire, add 1 cup chicken stock, and cook until it is reduced by one half. Add 1 tablespoon meat glaze (Bovril), 1 cup crème fraîche (see page 160) that has been mixed with 1 teaspoon potato flour, and allow to reduce again until the sauce is the consistency of heavy cream. Taste and correct the seasoning. Poach 1 to 2 cups Olympia oysters in their own liquid for 5 seconds, drain, and add to the sauce. This much can be prepared ahead. When ready to serve, reheat the sauce gently and spoon generously over the chicken. If Olympia oysters are not available, you may substitute large oysters, but be sure to cut them into 25-cent-size pieces.

Tomatoes Filled with Green Peas

CUT the tops off 6 firm, red tomatoes. Scoop out the centers carefully, sprinkle with salt, and turn upside down on towels to drain. Shell 2 pounds fresh green peas and cook according to the Paul Mayer method (see page 159) until barely tender. Drain and return the peas to the saucepan and add ¼ pound unsalted butter. Place the tomatoes on a cookie sheet and put into a 350-degree oven for 5 minutes. Remove from the oven and fill with the hot peas. Keep warm until ready to serve.

Mousse au Chocolat

IN A double boiler over simmering, not boiling water,

melt 4 ounces semisweet chocolate, a pinch of salt, 4 tablespoons sugar, ½ teaspoon vanilla, and 2 ounces unsalted butter, stirring constantly. When well blended, remove from the heat and stir in 4 egg yolks. Fold in very carefully—for this is the key to the lightness of the mousse —6 stiffly beaten egg whites and 1 cup whipped cream. Spoon into individual dishes and chill.

SHOPPING LIST

4-lb. capon cut into
   8 pieces
2 bunches broccoli
1 bunch celery
¼ lb. mushrooms
6 tomatoes
2 lbs. fresh peas

1 pt. heavy cream
4-oz. carton sour cream
1 package semisweet
   chocolate
1 to 2 jars Olympia
   oysters

STAPLES

sugar
olive oil
lemons (3)
garlic
parsley
butter (¾ lb.)
onion
chicken stock

meat glaze (Bovril)
potato flour
eggs (6)

salt
pepper
vanilla extract

Coquilles-Saint Jacques

(Scallops)

Roast Boned Leg of Lamb

Torta di Melanzana

(Eggplant Pie)

Watercress and Endive Salad

Fresh Strawberry Soufflé

WINE
With the scallops, a white Bordeaux, Entre-Deux-Mers, and with the lamb, a red Bordeaux, a Graves, or a California Gamay.

TO SERVE 8

REMARKS

THIS was the menu I chose to do for my first class. I wanted an impressive meal, and everyone was indeed impressed to see how easy it is to prepare an elegant meal in advance. The Coquille is a popular way to serve scallops; the lamb, roasted quickly and served rare, is succulent and tender; and the strawberry soufflé maintains a fresh strawberry taste. I am sure your guests will be as delighted with this dinner as my students were.

METHOD

FINISH preparing the scallops and gently reheat them just before your guests arrive. Spoon them into shells and place the shells on a cookie sheet, ready to go into the oven. The scallops make a good hors d'oeuvre served about midway in the cocktail hour. Before the guests arrive, finish roasting the lamb and leave in a warm place, covered loosely with foil until ready to carve on the bias and serve. Allowing about an hour cooking time, pour the custard over the eggplant, and put it into the oven. As soon as the eggplant is finished, invite your guests to the table and then serve the meal. When the last guest has finished, remove the dinner plates, whisk the egg whites for the soufflé, then carefully fold them into the strawberry base. (The base may be made several hours ahead.) Put the soufflé into the oven, noting the time, and bring the salad with its dressing to the table. Toss and serve the salad, and by the time it is finished and the table is cleared, your soufflé will be ready. Have the plates, spoons, and forks for the soufflé, a trivet, and a large serving spoon waiting on the table. Bring in the soufflé and enjoy the compliments.

Coquilles Saint-Jacques

(Scallops)

Bring to a boil 1½ cups dry white wine with a bouquet garni (see page 158). Add 1 pound scallops, washed and drained, and a pinch of salt, and simmer for 1 minute. Drain the scallops, reserving the broth, and cut them into small, uniform pieces. Clean and chop ½ pound fresh mushrooms. Put them into a saucepan with 6 finely chopped shallots and 1 tablespoon finely chopped parsley. Add 2 tablespoons butter, 1 teaspoon lemon juice, and 2 tablespoons water. Cover and simmer for 10 minutes. Strain and add the liquor to the wine broth. Melt 4 tablespoons butter in a saucepan and add 4 tablespoons flour, stir with a wire whisk, add gradually the combined hot liquors, and cook, stirring constantly until the sauce is thickened and smooth. Add 3 or 4 tablespoons heavy cream. Correct the seasoning and stir in the scallops, shallots, mushrooms, and ½ pound cooked tiny shrimp. Just before serving, reheat, spoon into individual scallop shells, piling high in the center, and put into a preheated 450-degree oven for 5 minutes.

Roast Boned Leg of Lamb

Have your butcher bone and leave flat a 5-pound leg of lamb. In a glass or enameled container marinate it in the following mixture: In a medium saucepan, put ¾ cup dry white wine, ¾ cup Japanese soy sauce, 1 tablespoon powdered ginger, 1 tablespoon sugar, 2 crushed cloves of garlic, and ½ teaspoon crushed peppercorns. Bring to a boil and boil 1 minute. Cool and pour over the lamb. Marinate 2 or 3 hours. When ready to roast, pour off the marinade and put the lamb into a 450-degree preheated oven for 25 minutes for rare. Then put it under an extremely hot broiler or on the barbecue for 3 minutes each side to char. Let rest in a warm place at least 20 minutes before slicing and serving.

Torta di Melanzana
(Eggplant Pie)

OVER a high flame fry slices of eggplant in hot oil until they are soft and delicately browned. Place a layer of eggplant slices in a large, flat pie dish or long Pyrex dish, and season with salt, pepper, finely minced parsley, and dried thyme. Cover with a layer of sliced tomatoes. Sprinkle with salt, pepper, parsley, finely chopped onion, and chopped green pepper. Cover the tomatoes with thin slices of Mozzarella cheese. Beat 3 egg yolks into 1½ cups light cream and, 45 minutes before serving, pour over entire dish and bake uncovered in a 325-degree oven until done. To serve, cut like a pie.

Salad

A WATERCRESS and endive salad with mustard dressing (see Basic Recipes, pages 162–163).

Fresh Strawberry Soufflé

PREPARE the soufflé dish (see page 161) and set aside. Melt 3 tablespoons butter in a saucepan, add 2 tablespoons flour, blend well, and cook until the mixture begins to boil. Add ½ cup warm milk and continue cooking, stirring constantly with a wire sauce whisk, for 3 or 4 minutes. Remove the pot from the fire and add 5 egg yolks that have been beaten lightly with 3 tablespoons sugar. Then add 1 cup finely chopped fresh ripe strawberries that have been mixed with 2 tablespoons of sugar and sprinkled with a little brandy. This much can be done several hours ahead. Thirty minutes before serving, whisk 6 egg whites until they are stiff and add 2 teaspoons sugar. Continue whisking for a moment. Then fold the egg whites into the strawberry mixture. Pour the batter into the prepared soufflé dish and bake in a 400-degree oven for 20 to 25 minutes. Serve immediately.

SHOPPING LIST

½ lb. tiny cooked shrimp
1 lb. scallops
5-lb. leg of lamb, boned
   and left open
½ lb. mushrooms
6 shallots
1 medium-sized eggplant
4 ripe tomatoes
1 green pepper
2 bunches watercress

1 head of French endive
1 pt. ripe strawberries
½ pt. heavy cream
1 pt. light cream
small bottle Japanese
   soy sauce
5 slices Mozzarella
   cheese
dry white wine
brandy

STAPLES

butter
sugar
lemon
garlic
flour
vegetable oil
parsley
onion
white wine vinegar

Dijon mustard
eggs (12)
milk
salt
pepper
powdered ginger
thyme
bouquet garni (see page 158)

81

Cream of Butter Lettuce Soup

Veal Kidneys in Madeira Wine

Pommes au Beurre

Lime Pie

WINE
*A dry red Médoc or
California Cabernet
Sauvignon. With dessert, a*
TO SERVE 8   *Barsac or Cream Sherry.*

THIS is a delicate, elegant meal, and my favorite way of preparing kidneys. The soup is an unusual and delicious way of serving a salad and the lime pie is refreshing. This is an easy menu to cook and serve. Lamb kidneys may be substituted for veal if desired.

METHOD

PREPARE the soup well ahead and reheat to serve. The kidneys may also be finished before your guests arrive and reheated gently (being careful not to overcook the kidneys) just before serving. The pie needs at least 2 hours chilling time.

Cream of Butter Lettuce Soup

BRING a cup of chicken stock to the boil, and add 2 large or 4 small washed heads of butter lettuce. Boil for 5 minutes. In a small saucepan melt 3 tablespoons butter, add 3 tablespoons flour, cook 2 minutes, and gradually stir in 1½ cups milk. Continue cooking until the béchamel thickens. If it is too thick, add a little chicken stock; if it is too thin, let it simmer a little longer. Add salt and pepper to taste. Lift out the lettuce and put it into the container of the blender, add the béchamel and a cup of sour cream. Blend everything briefly. Return soup to a saucepan and gently reheat, while you adjust flavor, seasoning, and thickness. Use as much chicken stock, tablespoon by tablespoon, as is needed to thin the soup to your personal taste.

Veal Kidneys in Madeira Wine

CUT 4 veal kidneys in half and remove the fat and tubes.

83

Then cut each half in about 3 pieces. Heat 3 tablespoons butter in a heavy skillet until it turns brown. Flour the kidney pieces lightly, spanking off any excess flour, and sauté them for 5 minutes on each side over medium heat. Remove them and add 24 mushrooms cut in quarters and cook over high heat for 1 minute. Remove mushrooms from pan. Meanwhile, in another skillet, sauté 16 tiny pork sausages cut in half for about 10 minutes until done. Drain on paper towels. Pour off the excess butter from the skillet in which you browned the kidneys and mushrooms. Add 1 tablespoon meat glaze (Bovril) that has been blended with 1 tablespoon potato flour. Add gradually 1 cup beef stock (see page 158) and 1 cup Madeira wine. Stir over a medium flame until it boils, scraping up all the brown bits left by the kidneys. Cook until the sauce thickens somewhat. Strain the sauce and taste for seasoning. Return the kidneys, mushrooms, and sausages to the pan, and add the sauce. Just before serving, heat through, being careful not to overcook the kidneys, and serve in a small casserole garnished with freshly minced parsley.

Pommes au Beurre

PARBOIL 4 potatoes cut into small potato shapes (balls, ovals, etc.) for 5 minutes in salted water and drain them well. Sauté them to a rich golden brown in a generous amount of clarified butter (see page 159). Season to taste with salt and pepper.

Lime Pie

PREPARE a tart pastry (see page 163), chill and roll out to about ⅛ inch. Line an 8-inch tart tin with the pastry. Beat 3 egg yolks until thick, add 1 can sweetened condensed milk and ¾ cup freshly squeezed lime juice. Fold in 3 stiffly beaten egg whites and pour into the tart shell. Place the pie on the bottom of a 425-degree gas oven for

10 minutes or over the coils on top of an electric stove for 7 minutes, in order to brown the lower crust. Reduce oven heat to 350 degrees and finish baking on the rack for 10 to 15 minutes more. Serve chilled, garnished with whipped cream.

SHOPPING LIST

4 veal kidneys, very light in color	6 limes
16 tiny pork sausages	½ pt. sour cream
2 large heads of butter lettuce	1 can sweetened condensed milk
24 mushrooms	½ pt. heavy cream
	Madeira wine

STAPLES

chicken stock	beef stock
butter	parsley
flour	eggs
milk	
meat glaze (Bovril)	salt
potato flour	pepper

Fresh Salmon Soufflé

Marinated Roast Beef

Sauce Poivrade

Potatoes Boulangère

Watercress Salad

Chocolate Fudge Pie

TO SERVE 8

WINE
*A full-bodied red,
Saint-Emilion or Cent-Vignes
or a California Cabernet
Sauvignon.*

Don't be put off if at first glance this menu seems too rich. The fresh salmon soufflé is an exciting first course and the sauce for the beef is unusual. There was a highly critical student in one of my classes who was able to find something wrong with every dish I served. The fudge pie on this menu is so good I wondered what she would find to criticize about it. It amused me when, after finishing every crumb of the pie, her criticism was "a pinch too much salt in the pastry crust."

METHOD

The pie should be made in the morning and chilled. Be careful not to overbake it—it should be soft and fudgy. The salmon soufflé base can be prepared ahead and left to wait. The meat should be roasted and taken out of the oven to be kept warm, sauce already made, when the guests arrive. The potatoes should be cooked and kept in a warm place. After the last guest arrives put the soufflé into the oven. Be sure to note the time carefully, perhaps announcing, as I do, that there is a soufflé in the oven and everyone has to be seated in exactly 20 minutes. After that, my guests watch the time for me. When everyone is seated, bring the soufflé to the table and serve. Serve the beef, sliced thinly on the diagonal, with some sauce, and pass extra sauce for those who wish it. A salad of watercress with a mustard dressing is just right served next. The fudge pie is so rich, small slices will do.

Fresh Salmon Soufflé

Grind twice, with the finest blade of your grinder, 1½ pounds salmon fillet. In a small saucepan melt 3 teaspoons

87

butter. Remove from the heat and add 2 teaspoons flour. Season to taste with salt, cayenne pepper, ½ teaspoon dry mustard, 1 teaspoon dried dill weed, and blend in ⅓ cup milk. Return the sauce to the flame and stir constantly with a wire sauce whisk until it boils. Remove from the heat and add 2 tablespoons sherry wine. Mix this sauce with the raw fish. This much can be prepared well ahead. Approximately 25 to 30 minutes before serving, fold in very carefully 1 cup stiffly whipped cream and 5 stiffly whisked egg whites. Spoon the mixture into a well-greased 2-quart soufflé dish and bake 25 minutes in a preheated 375-degree oven.

Marinated Roast Beef

SELECT a 3- to 4-pound piece of your favorite cut of beef—filet, butterball, Châteaubriand, etc. Place the meat in the following marinade 2 hours before roasting: Combine 1 cup red wine, ½ cup tarragon vinegar, ½ teaspoon thyme, a bay leaf, 6 whole cloves, a sliced carrot and a sliced onion and 1 clove of minced garlic. When ready to roast, remove the meat from the marinade (reserving marinade) and put into a 450-degree oven, allowing 8 minutes a pound for rare. Let stand in a warm place at least 20 minutes before carving thinly on the bias. Serve with Sauce Poivrade.

Sauce Poivrade

COOK ½ cup chopped carrots, ½ cup chopped onions, and a bouquet garni (see page 158) in butter until softened. Drain off the butter, add ¼ cup tarragon vinegar and ½ cup of the strained meat marinade to the vegetables, and cook over a high heat until it is two thirds of its original volume, stirring constantly. Add 1½ cups brown sauce (see below) and simmer for 30 minutes. Add 8 crushed black peppercorns and simmer gently 10 minutes more. Correct the seasoning, strain, and just before serving bring to a boil and stir in 2 tablespoons butter.

Brown Sauce

IN A saucepan melt 1½ tablespoons butter, add 1½ tablespoons flour, and stir with a wire sauce whisk until thoroughly blended and brown in color. Add gradually 2 cups strong beef stock (page 158), bring to a boil, then lower the heat and simmer for 20 minutes. Strain.

Potatoes Boulangère

PEEL and slice 5 or 6 potatoes. Peel and slice 1 small onion as thinly as possible. Mix the potatoes and onion together and season with salt, pepper, and 1 tablespoon freshly minced parsley. Put the mixture into a well-buttered ovenproof container and spread 4 tablespoons softened unsalted butter over the top. Add 4 ounces or more of chicken stock until the liquid comes halfway up the sides of the dish. Bake in a 400-degree oven for 30 to 40 minutes, until the potatoes are soft and the liquid is absorbed.

Salad

A WATERCRESS salad with mustard dressing (see Basic Recipes, pages 162–163).

Chocolate Fudge Pie

PREPARE a tart pastry (see page 163), chill and roll out to about ⅛-inch thick. Line an 8-inch tart tin with the pastry. Cream ½ cup butter and add gradually 1 cup sugar. Add 1 teaspoon vanilla and blend thoroughly. Add 2 egg yolks, beating well after each addition. Add 2 squares melted bitter chocolate, then add ½ cup sifted flour. Whisk

2 egg whites with a pinch of salt until they are stiff and fold into the chocolate mixture. Turn the filling into the pastry shell and place the pie on the bottom of a 425-degree gas oven for 10 minutes or over the coils on top of an electric stove for 7 minutes, in order to brown the lower crust. Reduce oven heat to 350 degrees and finish baking on the rack for 10 to 15 minutes more. Decorate with chopped pistachios and chill.

SHOPPING LIST

1½ lbs. salmon fillet
3- to 4-lb. beef roast,
    (filet, butterball, etc.)
1 bunch carrots
2 bunches watercress
1 pt. heavy cream

2-oz. package bitter
    chocolate
2 oz. pistachio nuts
sherry
red wine

STAPLES

butter
sugar
flour
milk
eggs
vegetable oil
onions
garlic
beef stock (2 cups), see
    page 158
potatoes (5–6)
parsley
chicken stock

tarragon vinegar

dry mustard
Dijon mustard
dried dill weed
thyme
bayleaf
cloves
black peppercorns
salt
pepper
cayenne pepper
bouquet garni (page 158)

Shrimp and Oyster Bisque

Sweetbreads in a Truffle Sauce

Tomatoes with Spinach Purée

Butter Lettuce and Parsley Salad

Fresh Raspberry Soufflé, Sauce Parisienne

WINE
White Bordeaux: Graves,
White Burgundy: Pouilly-Fuissé,
or a California Pinot
Chardonnay.

TO SERVE 6

REMARKS

THIS is an elegant, rich dinner and one of the slightly more complicated to prepare. The sauce in which the sweetbreads are served is a combination of cream, white port, Madeira, and truffles, a heavenly blend of ingredients. The trick of the exceptional raspberry soufflé is that the flavor and texture of the fresh raspberries is held by sealing them with sugar syrup and giving them a minimum of cooking. For an appreciative audience, this menu is well worth the effort. Boned chicken breasts may be substituted for the sweetbreads; simply eliminate the blanching step.

METHOD

BLANCH and skin the sweetbreads and press them between two plates the day or morning before the dinner. The bisque may be prepared several hours ahead and reheated just before serving. Finish preparing the sweetbreads completely before the guests arrive, gently reheating just before serving. Have the spinach in the tomatoes ready to place in the oven when the bisque is served. Follow the method on page 161 for the soufflé.

Shrimp and Oyster Bisque

CHOP finely 2 cups each of shucked oysters and shelled, raw shrimp. Reserve the oyster liquor. Put the oysters, shrimp, and oyster liquor in a heavy soup pot; add 4 cups milk, 1 cup heavy cream, ½ cup peeled minced celery, 3 tablespoons finely minced shallots, 1 tablespoon minced parsley, a pinch of mace, salt and pepper to taste. Simmer for 30 minutes. Put through a food mill or sieve. In a saucepan melt 3 tablespoons unsalted butter, stir in 3 tablespoons flour, and cook for 3 or 4 minutes. Stir into the bisque. One or 2 egg yolks may be added for increased richness.

Sweetbreads in a Truffle Sauce

THE preliminary preparation for sweetbreads is always the same. Soak the sweetbreads in cold water for an hour. Simmer them for 5 minutes in water to which the juice of a lemon has been added. Put them into ice water to stop their cooking and very carefully remove all of the membrane, fat, and tubing. Then press the sweetbreads between two plates with a weight on top to flatten them. Refrigerate for several hours.

Flour 3 pounds sweetbreads, spanking off the excess flour, and sauté them in foaming butter for 10 minutes on each side. Remove them from heat and keep warm on a serving platter. Drain away the excess butter from the pan and add 1 cup heavy cream, 1 cup white port wine, and 1 cup Madeira wine. Add as many thinly sliced truffles with their juice as you can afford. Reduce the sauce to the consistency of heavy, thick cream. Gently warm the sweetbreads in the sauce, and serve.

Tomatoes with Spinach Purée

SLICE off the tops of 6 firm ripe tomatoes. Scoop out the pulp, sprinkle the shells with salt and pepper, and turn upside down to drain. Meanwhile make the spinach purée. Place the tomato shells on a greased cookie sheet, put a dot of butter in each, and place in a 350-degree oven for 5 minutes. Remove, allow to cool slightly, and fill with hot spinach purée. Return to the oven for 5 minutes more and serve.

Spinach Purée

PLACE 2 cups cooked, chopped spinach in the container of a blender. Add ½ to 1 cup béchamel sauce (see below), spoon by spoon, and blend. Season to taste with salt, pepper, and nutmeg.

Béchamel Sauce

MELT 4 tablespoons unsalted butter, add 4 tablespoons flour, stir together, and cook for 5 minutes. Add 1½ cups or more of milk and cook until thickened.

Salad

A BUTTER lettuce and parsley salad with herb dressing (see Basic Recipes, page 162).

Fresh Raspberry Soufflé

MEASURE 14 level tablespoons sugar into a heavy saucepan. Add 1 tablespoon water and bring to a solid boil, stirring continuously with a wooden spoon to prevent the sugar from burning. Continue boiling until it reaches the "hard-ball" stage or until a candy thermometer reads between 250 and 255 degrees. This must be exact. Remove immediately from the heat and stir in 1 pound fresh raspberries. This much may be prepared ahead. Whisk 6 egg whites with ½ teaspoon cream of tartar. Quickly and carefully fold into the raspberries, pour into a prepared soufflé dish (page 161), and bake at 425 degrees for 15 to 20 minutes.

Sauce Parisienne

MIX ½ cup vanilla sauce (see below) with ½ cup puréed fresh raspberries. Fold in 1 cup whipped cream. Spoon over each serving of soufflé.

Vanilla Sauce

SCALD ½ cup each milk and heavy cream with 1 teaspoon vanilla extract. Beat 2 egg yolks with ¼ cup sugar and combine with the hot milk and cream, stirring with a whisk. Cook, stirring constantly, until the mixture thickens. Strain through a fine sieve and let cool.

SHOPPING LIST

2 doz. oysters in their shells *or*
2 8-oz. jars shucked oysters
¾ lb. raw shrimp
3 lbs. veal sweetbreads
1 stalk celery
3 shallots

6 tomatoes
2 lbs. spinach
2 heads butter lettuce
3 pts. fresh raspberries
2 pts. heavy cream
truffles, 1 or 2
white port wine
Madeira wine

STAPLES

milk (5 cups)
parsley
butter
flour
eggs (8)
vegetable oil
tarragon wine vinegar
sugar

lemon

mace
salt
pepper
cream of tartar
vanilla extract
nutmeg

95

Gravlax
(Swedish Marinated Salmon)

Lihamurekepüras
(Meat Loaf in Pastry Crust)

Agurkesalat
(Cucumber Salad)

Apricot Mousse

WINE
A French medium Burgundy such as a Pommard or a California Pinot Noir.

THE first time this Scandinavian menu was prepared in class, a woman commented that she was Norwegian and one of the things she was happy to have left in Norway was the salted fish and pickled cucumbers. She continued that she had never eaten the fish and the cucumbers were always soggy. I didn't know quite how to respond and, embarrassed, continued preparing the meal. I was delighted when, after eating, she made a point of saying how much she regretted having not eaten gravlax all those years and how tasty and crisp she had found the cucumbers. Indeed, this is a delicious and lovely looking dinner.

METHOD

AGAIN, everything should be prepared in advance. When the last guest arrives, I put the meat loaf into the oven, noting the time carefully. When it is taken out, transfer it immediately to a cutting board and let it stand in a warm place. The salmon, sliced and arranged in thin, overlapping slices on individual plates, can be on the table when the guests sit down. The mustard sauce is passed. The meat loaf, in its shiny crust, is a beautiful display to bring to the table. It must be sufficiently rested so that it does not fall apart when sliced—at least 20 minutes out of the oven. Sour cream and lingonberries, already on the table, may be passed. The cucumbers are served with the meat but on separate plates. The apricot mousse comes to the table any time you are ready.

Gravlax
(Swedish Marinated Salmon)

HAVE your fish dealer bone and cut in half lengthwise a 2½-pound center cut of fresh salmon. Place half the fish, skin side down, in a deep glass container. Wash and shake dry a bunch of fresh dill and place it on the fish. Combine ¼ cup coarse salt, ¼ cup sugar, and 2 tablespoons crushed peppercorns. Sprinkle this mixture evenly over the dill, then moisten with 1 teaspoon white vinegar. Top with the other half of the fish, skin side up; cover with foil and place a weight on top. Refrigerate 2 or 3 days, turning the fish every 12 hours, basting with the liquid marinade that accumulates. When the fish is finished, remove from the marinade, rinse away the seasonings, and pat it dry. Place the separated halves skin side down and slice the salmon halves thinly on the diagonal. Serve with toast, lemon wedges, freshly ground pepper, and mustard sauce.

Mustard Sauce

IN A blender container place 4 tablespoons Dijon mustard, 1 teaspoon dry mustard, 3 tablespoons chopped fresh dill, 3 tablespoons sugar, and 2 tablespoons white vinegar. Run blender a few seconds until mixture is a paste and then slowly pour in ⅓ cup vegetable oil until it forms a thick mayonnaise.

Lihamurekepüras
(Meat Loaf in Pastry Crust)

PREPARE the sour cream pastry on page 163, and chill. Sauté ¼ pound finely chopped mushrooms in 2 tablespoons foaming butter until soft. Set aside and in the same skillet sauté 1 pound ground lean beef, 1 pound ground lean pork, and 1 pound ground veal. With a slotted spoon, draining the mixture of fat as you go, transfer the cooked meat and mushrooms into a large mixing bowl. Stir in ⅓ cup finely chopped onions, ¼ cup finely chopped parsley, 1 cup freshly grated imported Swiss cheese, and ½ cup milk. Combine and season with salt and pepper to taste. Cut the chilled pastry dough in half and roll out

98

each half to a rectangle 6 by 14 inches, reserving any scraps. Butter an inverted cookie sheet; lift one sheet of the pastry over the rolling pin and onto the pan. Now place the meat mixture in the center of the dough. Pat the meat into a narrow loaf extending down the center of the dough. Gently drape the second sheet of pastry on top of the meat loaf and press the edges together with the tines of a fork. Roll out the scraps and cut into long narrow strips and decorate the top of the loaf. Brush the pastry with 1 egg combined with 2 tablespoons milk and place in a preheated 375-degree oven for approximately 45 minutes or until the loaf has turned a golden brown. Serve thick slices of the hot loaf, accompanied by a bowl of sour cream and a side dish of lingonberries.

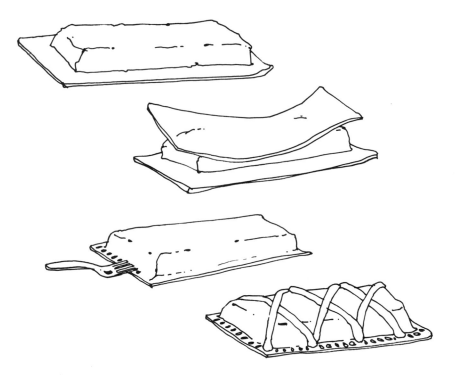

99

Agurkesalat
(Cucumber Salad)

SCORE 4 large cucumbers, cut them in half lengthwise, and seed them with a teaspoon. Cut them into the thinnest possible slices and place in a single layer on paper towels. Sprinkle with salt, place more towels on top and a weight on top of the towels for an hour or so. Then remove the weight and gently pat the cucumbers dry with fresh towels. Place the slices in a shallow glass dish and pour over them the following marinade: Beat together 1¼ cups white vinegar, 2 tablespoons sugar, 1 teaspoon salt, and ½ teaspoon pepper. Chill and drain away the liquid before serving.

Apricot Mousse

SIMMER 1 pound dried apricots in water to cover for 25 minutes. Stir in ½ cup sugar or more to taste and cook the fruit for 5 more minutes. Purée the apricots in a blender. Add ¼ pound melted unsalted butter. Stir in ¼ cup slivered toasted almonds. Whip 1 cup heavy cream and sweeten it to taste with sugar and vanilla. Fold the whipped cream into the puréed apricots and pour the mousse into small dessert dishes. Chill thoroughly.

SHOPPING LIST

2½ lb. center-cut salmon fillet	1 jar preserved lingonberries
1 lb. ground lean beef	¼ lb. mushrooms
1 lb. ground lean pork	4 cucumbers
1 lb. ground veal	thinly sliced white bread
1 pt. sour cream	1 lb. dried apricots
8 oz. imported Swiss cheese	4 oz. slivered blanched almonds
½ pt. heavy cream	

STAPLES

sugar
white cider vinegar
   (1½ cups)
lemons
Dijon mustard
vegetable oil
flour
butter
eggs
onions

parsley
milk

fresh dill
coarse salt
   (kosher salt)
peppercorns
dry mustard
salt
vanilla extract

Consommé Bruxelles

(Consommé with Brussels Sprouts)

Turban of Sole Carmélite

Pommes Nouvelles

Butter Lettuce Salad

Frozen Lemon Cream

WINE
A Meursault or a California Sémillon

TO SERVE 6

THE simple clear soup with Brussels sprouts is an understated beginning to this rich, elegant dinner. The ring of salmon and sole with artichoke hearts, mushrooms, and shrimp in a béchamel sauce is an intoxicating dish. The frozen lemon cream is refreshingly tart but sweet and rich at the same time. This is an often requested meal by students and friends and a relatively easy and quick one to prepare.

METHOD

FINISH preparing the soup, leaving the Brussels sprouts separate until ready to reheat and serve. The turban may be prepared hours ahead and placed in the refrigerator to wait for its final baking. The vegetables and shrimp can wait in the béchamel until time to reheat and serve. Thirty-five minutes before serving, put the turban into the oven. Let it rest 10 minutes before unmolding. The frozen lemon cream must be made well ahead and served frozen.

Consommé Bruxelles
(Consommé with Brussels Sprouts)

WASH 24 tiny Brussels sprouts and remove the outer leaves. Cook the sprouts according to the Paul Mayer method (see page 159) until barely tender. Heat 5 cups homemade chicken stock and add ¼ cup of the water in which the sprouts were cooked. Put 4 sprouts in each soup plate and pour the hot consommé over them. Grated Parmesan cheese may be passed with the soup.

Turban of Sole Carmélite

CUT 4 thin fillets of salmon from a fillet weighing 1¼ pounds, and prepare a mousseline forcemeat (see below) with the rest of the fish. Line a buttered ring mold with the 4 fillets of salmon and 4 fillets of sole that have been divided into 8 pieces. If possible, let the fillets hang over the outside of the mold. Spoon the forcemeat gently into the mold and fold the ends of the fillets over it. Press

buttered wax paper over the mold and bake in a larger pan of hot water in a 400-degree oven for 25 minutes.

Cook ½ pound raw shrimp barely covered in half dry white wine and half water until they turn pink, about 30 seconds. Remove the shrimp, shell, devein, and set aside. Strain the liquid through a cloth and reserve. Sauté ¼ pound mushroom caps and 6 previously cooked small artichoke bottoms cut in half, in butter for 1 minute. In a heavy saucepan melt 3 tablespoons butter. Add 3 tablespoons flour, stirring constantly. Cook over a medium flame for 2 minutes and add ½ cup of the reserved shrimp liquid and about ¾ cup light cream, stirring constantly. Cook until the sauce thickens to the consistency of very thick cream. Combine the shrimp, artichoke bottoms, and mushrooms and add to the sauce. Unmold the turban onto a heated platter and fill the center with the shrimp and vegetable mixture. Garnish with watercress.

Mousseline Forcemeat

Run the remaining salmon fillet, about ¾ pound, through the fine blade of a food chopper. Add ¼ teaspoon salt and a little white pepper. Gradually add the whites of 2 eggs, stirring vigorously with a wooden spoon. Place the bowl over cracked ice and gradually, using the wooden spoon, work in 1½ cups heavy cream. The mixture should be light and fluffy.

Pommes Nouvelles

Scrub the skins from 24 tiny new potatoes. Parboil in salted water for 3 minutes and dry them well. Heat 6 tablespoons butter in a heavy skillet, add the potatoes, salt and pepper, and cook until they are tender and golden brown all over. Sprinkle with finely chopped parsley just before serving.

Salad

For a butter lettuce and parsley salad, see Basic Recipes, page 162.

Frozen Lemon Cream

Stir 1 cup milk, 1 cup heavy cream, and 1 cup sugar together until the sugar is thoroughly dissolved. Pour the mixture into a refrigerator tray and freeze it until it is mushy. Add the grated rind and juice of 3 lemons, beat the mixture well with a rotary beater, and freeze it again for 2 hours. Beat the cream again thoroughly, return it to the freezer and freeze it until it is solid. The lemon cream may be served in scooped out lemon shells or long-stemmed sherbet glasses. Garnish with a lemon leaf.

SHOPPING LIST

1¼ lbs. salmon fillet
4 fillets of sole
½ pound raw shrimp
24 Brussels sprouts
¼ lb. mushrooms
6 small artichokes
1 bunch watercress

24 small new potatoes
1½ pts. heavy cream
½ pt. light cream
¼ lb. Parmesan
   cheese (optional)
dry white wine

STAPLES

chicken stock (5 cups)
butter
flour
eggs
parsley
sugar (1 cup)
milk

lemons (3)
6 lemons for serving
   (optional)

salt
white pepper

Shrimp Sauté

Caneton au Grand Marnier

(Duckling in Grand Marnier Sauce)

Pommes de Terre à la Parisienne

(Potatoes Parisienne)

Glazed Onions

Plum Milk Sherbet

WINE
*A French Volnay or a
California Red Burgundy.*

REMARKS

My objection to so many orange duckling recipes is that they are generally too sweet. I think, however, that you will find this is not the case with Caneton au Grand Marnier, a classic and very popular French dish. The plum milk sherbet is most unusual and a not-too-sweet end to this meal.

METHOD

HAVE the shrimp peeled and waiting next to the skillet with melted butter and parsley. Two minutes before serving, sauté quickly. The shrimp served in scallop shells make good hors d'oeuvre. The duck can be prepared ahead and left waiting in its sauce to be reheated. Do the same with the onions and potatoes. The plum sherbet is ready when you are, and is attractive served in long-stemmed glasses.

Shrimp Sauté

PEEL and devein 1 pound raw shrimp. Rinse and dry gently with a paper towel. In a large skillet heat 4 tablespoons unsalted butter and when it foams, add 3 tablespoons finely chopped parsley. Add the shrimp and sauté them for about 1 minute or until they are pink. Do not overcook them as they become tough and rubbery. Season with salt and pepper, and sprinkle with fresh lemon juice. Serve in scallop shells.

Caneton au Grand Marnier
(Duckling in Grand Marnier Sauce)

TRIM the wing tips and cut off the necks of 2 ducklings. Out of the wing tips, neck, and giblets, excluding the liver,

108

make a duck stock (see page 159). Cut the ducklings into quarters, sprinkle with salt and pepper, and place them skin side up on a rack in a shallow roasting pan. Roast in a 400-degree oven, basting frequently with the fat that accumulates in the pan, about 1 hour or until done. Remove the ducklings from the pan and set in a warm place. Add 1 tablespoon unsalted butter to ½ cup duck stock, fat removed, add the grated rind of 1 orange, 1 cup sliced raw mushrooms, and 1 small clove of crushed garlic. Bring the mixture to a boil and simmer it gently for 2 minutes. Remove the pan from the heat and blend in 2 tablespoons potato flour mixed to a paste with 2 tablespoons duck stock. Stir in ¼ cup each dry sherry and cognac and ¾ cups each Grand Marnier and orange juice. Return the pan to the heat and cook, stirring with a wire sauce whisk, until the mixture is smooth and thickened. Add 1 teaspoon red currant jelly. Remove and discard the garlic and season to taste with salt and pepper. When ready to serve, heat the duck pieces well in the sauce. Arrange the duck on a serving platter and spoon over the sauce. Garnish with slices of orange.

Pommes de Terre à la Parisienne
(Potatoes Parisienne)

WITH a ball-cutter, scoop out potatoes in rounds smaller than hazelnuts. Sauté the potatoes in clarified butter (see page 159) until they are golden and soft. Sprinkle with chopped parsley and serve.

Glazed Onions

PEEL 24 small white onions and put them into a saucepan with 4 tablespoons melted butter. Add ¾ cup chicken stock, 1 tablespoon sugar, and ½ teaspoon salt, and let them cook very slowly, uncovered, over a low flame, until the onions are tender and the liquid is completely reduced.

Plum Milk Sherbet

BEAT 2 egg whites until they are stiff. Gradually beat in ¼ cup sugar, 2 cups milk, 1 cup corn syrup, and ⅔ cup lemon juice; transfer the mixture to a shallow dish and freeze. When the sherbet reaches the mushy stage, in about 2 hours, beat it again until it is smooth, then add 2 cups puréed cooked plums. Return it to the freezer and, when it is almost solid, beat it again until smooth. Cover the dish and freeze the sherbet once more until it is firm.

SHOPPING LIST

1 lb. raw shrimp	carrot ⎫
2 4-lb. ducklings	onion ⎬ for duck stock
5 juice oranges	celery ⎭
½ lb. mushrooms	dry Sherry
24 small white onions	cognac
1½ lbs. ripe plums	Grand Marnier
red currant jelly	
corn syrup	

STAPLES

butter	sugar
parsley	milk
garlic	lemons (4)
potato flour	
potatoes	salt
chicken stock	pepper
eggs	

Carrot and Leek Bisque

Roast Lamb, Sauce Béarnaise

Pommes de Terre Dauphine

(Deep-Fried Potato Puffs)

Butter Lettuce and Parsley Salad

Gâteau au Chocolat et Marrons

(Chocolate and Chestnut Cake)

WINE

*A young Burgundy like
Mâcon, a Beaujolais,
Moulin-à-Vent, or a Cabernet
Sauvignon or Charbono from
California.*

TO SERVE 8

REMARKS

THIS is an elegant dinner to serve your gourmet friends. Both the carrot bisque and the chestnut cake are unusual and the béarnaise sauce a superb complement to the lamb. One of the students in my classes commented in amazement that the potatoes are so professional that they looked and tasted as good as in a restaurant!

METHOD

THE cake may be finished several hours ahead and refrigerated. Finish preparing the soup and reheat it slowly before serving. Roast the meat and keep warm. The potatoes are best when served as soon as they are fried; however, if you wish, you may fry them in advance and place them on paper towels on a baking sheet in a barely warm oven—they keep nicely for an hour or so. The béarnaise reheats perfectly, as long as it is stirred constantly during reheating with a wire sauce whisk. When ready to serve the main course, arrange the lamb slices in the center of a serving dish, garnish with béarnaise, and surround with the potato puffs. Present at the table with extra béarnaise to pass. A butter lettuce and parsley salad is suggested.

Carrot and Leek Bisque

COMBINE in a heavy soup pot 6 peeled carrots and 4 leeks, washed thoroughly and cut into 1-inch pieces. Add 5 cups chicken stock and salt and pepper to taste. Cook the vegetables covered about an hour or until they are very soft. In the container of the blender put ½ cup coarsely chopped parsley, add the vegetables and their broth and blend until the soup is thick and smooth. Just before serving, heat the soup, turn off the flame and add 3 egg yolks and 3 tablespoons crème fraîche (see page 160), stirring constantly. Heat slowly, and serve garnished with minced parsley.

Roast Lamb

FOR the roast lamb use a 6-pound leg of lamb or a 4-pound boned leg or three 2-pound racks of lamb. Preheat the oven for 30 minutes to 450 degrees, and have the lamb at room temperature. Rub the meat with a little olive oil, sprinkle with salt and pepper and place in the oven. For a 6-pound leg, 60 minutes is sufficient for rare; a 4-pound boned leg, left open and flat, 35 minutes for rare; a 2-pound rack, 25 minutes is adequate time for rare. For more well done, cook longer. When finished, remove the lamb from the roasting pan to the carving board, being careful not to pierce the meat, and let stand at least 20 minutes in a warm place before carving.

Sauce Béarnaise

COMBINE 1 cup dry white wine, 2 tablespoons tarragon vinegar, 1 tablespoon finely chopped shallots, ¼ teaspoon chervil, and 2 peppercorns. Cook over a high flame until reduced to two-thirds of its original volume. Cool a little before adding 3 egg yolks slowly, stirring constantly. Add ½ pound melted unsalted butter, little by little, stirring until the sauce has the consistency of heavy cream. Serve over the lamb. Note: In order to insure a smooth sauce, use a wire sauce whisk to stir the béarnaise.

Pommes de Terre Dauphine
(Deep-Fried Potato Puffs)

MAKE a mixture consisting of 2 cups of dry puréed

113

potatoes and an equal amount of pâte à choux (see below). Form little balls the size of a walnut, and drop into moderately hot fat to puff and brown. Drain on paper towels and serve hot.

Pâte à Choux

Combine in a saucepan 1 cup water, 2 tablespoons butter, and ½ teaspoon salt. Bring the mixture to the boil and add 1 cup flour, all at once, stirring well until the mixture leaves the sides of the pan. Remove from the fire and add, one at a time, 4 whole eggs, beating well with a wooden spoon after each addition. This batter should be very soft but not liquid. If necessary another egg may be added.

Salad

A butter lettuce and parsley salad with herb dressing (see page 162).

Gâteau au Chocolat et Marrons
(Chocolate and Chestnut Cake)

Melt 3 ounces semisweet chocolate with 4 tablespoons water. Separate 4 large eggs, and beat the yolks with 8 tablespoons sugar until thick. Add the chocolate and 8 ounces puréed chestnuts (see below). Whisk the 4 egg whites until stiff and fold into the chocolate mixture. Pour into two 8-inch greased and floured cake tins. Bake for 40 minutes at 350 degrees or until done (see page xix). Handle this cake very delicately, letting it cool in the pan approximately 10 minutes before removing to a cake rack. After cooling, assemble cake, using chocolate cream described below.

Chocolate Cream

MELT 3 ounces semisweet chocolate in 3 tablespoons water. Beat in 2 egg yolks, 2 tablespoons powdered sugar, and 1 tablespoon dark rum. Cool. Whip 1 cup cream until thick and fold into the chocolate. It looks good if the mixture is left rather streaky. Sandwich the cakes together with the chocolate cream, reserving some to spread over the top of the cake. Refrigerate until ready to serve.

Puréed Chestnuts

WITH a sharp knife, cut a slit on the convex sides of the shells of the chestnuts. Bake them on an oiled baking pan at 450 degrees for 5 or 6 minutes. When the chestnuts are cool enough to handle remove the shells with a sharp knife. Simmer them in milk until soft and then purée. Canned puréed chestnuts may be used when the fresh are not available.

SHOPPING LIST

6-lb. leg of lamb *or*
4-lb. boned leg,
   left open *or*
3 2-lb. racks of lamb
6 carrots
4 leeks
2 shallots
2 heads butter lettuce

1 pt. heavy cream
4 oz. sour cream
12 oz. fresh chestnuts *or*
  8 oz. canned puréed
   chestnuts
  6 oz. semisweet chocolate
dry white wine
dark rum

STAPLES

chicken stock (5 cups)
parsley
eggs (12)
olive oil
tarragon vinegar
butter (¾ lb.)
potatoes
vegetable oil

flour
sugar
powdered sugar

salt
pepper
chervil
whole peppercorns

115

A Holiday Dinner

Oyster Stew

Roast Turkey

Tarragon Stuffing, Spiced Sausage Stuffing

Giblet Sauce

Mashed Turnips with Butter

Cranberry Apples

Romaine Salad

Nancy Blinn's Dinner Rolls

Pumpkin Pie

WINE
*California Green Hungarian
or Ohio Catawba.*

TO SERVE 8 TO 12

REMARKS

FOR the past couple of years, my Thanksgiving dinners have included 25 to 30 people. Because of such a large group, a buffet had to be created. This same menu, with your own variations, appropriate to the occasion and the season, could be used for any festive gathering or holiday meal.

METHOD

THE day before, make the yeast dough and refrigerate. First thing in the morning, prepare the two stuffings, stuff turkey with both, and put it into the oven. Next, prepare the pastry crusts. While the pastry is chilling, make the pumpkin custard filling and the cranberry apples. Then roll out the pastry crusts and finish the pies. Peel and cook the turnips, mash with butter, and leave in the pot. Take the chilled yeast dough from the refrigerator, roll it out, and cut it into rolls. Let rise and when they have doubled in bulk, bake them. When the turkey is done, take it out of the oven and let it stand at least 1 hour before carving. When ready to carve, remove the stuffings and place them in attractive containers ready to reheat. Carve the turkey, arranging it on platters of all white meat and all dark meat. Covered with foil, the turkey stays succulent at room temperature until ready to serve. Prepare and chill the salad greens, make the salad dressing and the gravy for the turkey.

Since holidays are a family affair and include children, I invite my guests to come at five in the afternoon. Just before they arrive, everything is reheated except the turkey, which I prefer at room temperature. For a buffet, I arrange things on the table, with hot dishes on electric food warmers. At 6 P.M. everyone is invited to eat. Since each person helps himself, I am able to relax and enjoy the evening. For a large party, the oyster stew is eliminated only because service is difficult. For a small sit-down dinner, it is a wonderful addition to the menu.

Oyster Stew

COOK 2 to 3 dozen shucked oysters in their own liquor over a low flame for 2 minutes. Scald 6 cups light cream. Just before serving, reheat the cream and combine the oysters, their liquor, 3 tablespoons butter, salt, pepper, and cayenne to taste. Serve as the butter is melting.

Tarragon Stuffing

MAKE approximately 10 cups fresh white bread crumbs in the blender. Place 2 cups finely chopped shallots and 1 pound butter in a saucepan to melt. Add the bread crumbs, 2 tablespoons or more of chopped tarragon, ½ cup minced parsley, 1 teaspoon salt and pepper, or to taste, and mix well. If the stuffing is too dry, add a little chicken stock. Stuff the larger cavity of the turkey, place a piece of folded foil in the opening, and secure.

Spiced Sausage Stuffing

COMBINE the following ingredients: 2½ pounds lean ground pork, 1 finely chopped clove of garlic, ¼ cup finely chopped parsley, 1 teaspoon salt, ½ teaspoon Tabasco, ¼ teaspoon nutmeg, 1 teaspoon freshly ground black pepper, 1 teaspoon thyme, 1 tablespoon cognac. Blend well, fill the neck cavity of the turkey, and secure. If you have too much sausage stuffing, place the surplus in a covered casserole and bake separately.

121

Roast Turkey

FOR a 10- to 12-pound bird: Tie the legs securely, rub the turkey well with butter, and sprinkle with salt and pepper. Place the bird on its side and cover with a piece of cheesecloth. Roast the turkey on a rack in a shallow pan at 350 degrees for an hour. Baste and turn on its other side for an hour more, baste again and turn the bird on its back, breast side up, and roast approximately 1 hour and 20 minutes more. At each turn and baste step, the cheesecloth should remain over the top of the turkey. Allow about 20 minutes a pound all together. Baste often during this last period. If there are not enough pan juices for basting, add butter and white wine. Turkey is done when legs and thighs move up and down freely. Allow the turkey to settle in a warm place at least 1 hour before carving.

Giblet Sauce

POUR off all but 2 tablespoons of the pan drippings from the turkey. Add 2 cups chicken stock and deglaze the pan. Pour into a small saucepan, add the turkey giblets previously chopped and cooked until tender, and boil a few minutes to strengthen the flavor. Correct the seasoning, add 2 tablespoons of cognac, and reheat when ready to serve.

Mashed Turnips with Butter

PEEL and slice 10 turnips. Cook in boiling salted water until tender. Drain and mash with ½ pound butter. Add salt and freshly ground pepper to taste. Reheat when ready to serve.

Cranberry Apples

BOIL together, for 3 minutes, 1 cup each of cranberry

juice and sugar. Peel and dice 4 tart apples. Drop the apples a few at a time into the boiling syrup and cook them for about 6 minutes, or until just tender. Remove the fruit from the syrup and serve as a garnish with the turkey.

Salad

A ROMAINE lettuce salad with oil and vinegar dressing (see pages 162–163).

Nancy Blinn's Dinner Rolls

MIX 1 package dry yeast with 1 tablespoon warm water and 3 teaspoons sugar. Let stand 5 minutes. Scald and cool 1 cup milk. Cream together ½ cup butter and ¼ cup sugar, add 3 well-beaten eggs and the yeast mixture. Add 4 cups white flour alternately with the scalded milk. Let the dough stand in the mixing bowl in a warm place to rise. After 2 to 3 hours, punch it down, cover, and refrigerate overnight. Roll out and cut into round shapes, place on an ungreased cookie sheet, and let rise again. Bake in a 400-degree oven for 8 minutes. Makes approximately 3 dozen rolls.

Pumpkin Pie
(for 2 pies)

MAKE a tart pastry (see page 163) for 2 pies. Chill. Roll out to ⅛-inch thickness, and line two 8-inch buttered pie tins. Place 2 cups puréed pumpkin in a bowl and make a well in the center. Add 6 lightly beaten eggs combined with 2 cups heavy cream, ¼ teaspoon salt, ⅔ cup sugar, 1 teaspoon cinnamon, ¼ teaspoon ground cloves, ½ cup cognac, and ¼ teaspoon mace. Blend thoroughly. Correct the seasoning—you may want a spicier pie. Fill the pie shells and place the pies on the bottom of a 425-degree gas oven for 10 minutes or over the coils on top of an electric stove for 7 minutes, in order to brown the lower crust. Finish baking on the rack of a 350-degree oven about 10 minutes more until the custard is just set. Serve at room temperature with cognac-flavored and sweetened whipped cream.

SHOPPING LIST

2–3 doz. oysters

2½ lbs. lean ground pork

12-lb. turkey

1 lb. shallots

10 turnips

4 tart apples

3 heads romaine lettuce

1½ pts. heavy cream

3 pts. light cream

8 oz. cranberry juice

1-lb. can of pumpkin

1 package dry yeast

1 loaf French bread

cognac

dry white wine

Madeira wine

STAPLES

butter (2½ lbs.)

parsley

chicken stock

garlic

cheesecloth

vegetable oil

red wine vinegar

eggs (9)

sugar

milk

unbleached white flour
(6 cups)

salt

pepper

cayenne pepper

tarragon

thyme

cinnamon

ground cloves

ground mace

Tabasco

nutmeg

Large Buffet Dinners

Broiled Herbed Chicken Legs

Sliced Roast Veal with Mustard Sauce

Sausage Baked in Pastry

Steak Tartare

Marinated Mushrooms

Cucumbers in Sour Cream

Guacamole Salad

Assorted Breads, Toast and Crackers

Strawberry Bavarois

WINE
*Anything goes, a selection of
your favorite red and white
table wines*

TO SERVE 10

REMARKS

THIS is my most popular informal buffet dinner and one that adapts nicely to large crowds. By increasing the recipes, you may easily serve many more than 10. A tray of crisp raw vegetables, a cheese board, and bowls of fresh fruit may be added. With about an hour advance preparation time, this buffet, including the arrangement of the table, can be prepared in about 2 hours.

METHOD

THE first thing to be prepared on the day of the dinner is the pastry crust for the sausage. While it is chilling, assemble the strawberry bavarois and chill. After that, go right down the line, with the exception of the marinated mushrooms which should have been prepared at least 24 hours in advance. Leave the meats out at room temperature, and chill the salads. The entire buffet can be arranged on the table before the guests arrive. Dinner plates and cloth napkins wrapped around forks can be at one end of the table. If you have room on the buffet table, or perhaps on the table that serves as the bar, place an ice-filled bucket of splits of champagne, white wine, and bottles of beer for those not wishing hard liquor. An ice bucket, wine glasses, and bar glasses complete the arrangements. Your guests may now serve themselves.

Broiled Herbed Chicken Legs

PREPARE the following marinade: 1 cup vegetable oil, ½ cup lemon juice, 2 tablespoons minced tarragon, ¼ cup minced parsley, 2 crushed garlic cloves, ½ teaspoon salt, ½ teaspoon pepper.

An hour before broiling, pour the marinade over 10

128

chicken legs. Broil close to the flame, approximately 10 minutes each side. Drain marinade and serve chicken at room temperature.

Sliced Roast Veal

SELECT a 3-pound veal rib roast. Sprinkle with salt and pepper, spread with butter, and roast in a 350-degree oven 1½ hours or until the juices no longer run pink when the roast is pierced with a fork. Remove and allow to cool. Slice by the rib and arrange on a plate. Serve at room temperature with mustard sauce.

Mustard Sauce

CHOP 3 small sour pickles, 1 small sweet pickle, and a teaspoon of tarragon. Blend with ½ cup Dijon mustard and garnish with a little finely chopped pickle.

Sausage Baked in Pastry

PREPARE the sour cream pastry on page 163, and chill. Prick a 1- to 1½-pound uncooked French or Italian sausage in 5 or 6 places to prevent the skin from bursting. Place in a deep skillet and add enough cold water to cover. Bring to a boil and simmer, covered, for about an hour. Drain and cool the sausage on paper towels, then split the skin with a sharp knife and peel it off. To wrap the sausage in crust, roll out the pastry to a thickness of about ⅛ inch. Cut dough to the shape shown in Figure 1.

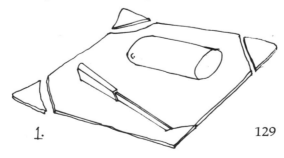

1.

Place sausage in the center of the dough, and gently lift the long sides of the pastry up over the sausage (Figure 2).

The pastry should overlap by about an inch; trim off anything more. Brush the edges with 1 egg beaten with a tablespoon of water and seal. Brush the ends of the roll with the egg and lift the flaps up and neatly seal (Figure 3).

Turn the wrapped sausage seam side down on a buttered baking sheet and decorate with the scraps of pastry dough cut into shapes (Figure 4).

Brush well with the rest of the egg mixture and bake at 375 degrees for 45 to 60 minutes until golden. Slice and serve with hot mustard.

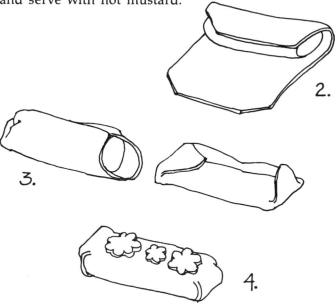

Steak Tartare

FOR 10 people you will need about a pound of lean beef. Use top round, sirloin, or tenderloin. Trim any visible fat and grind meat just before blending. Mix into the meat in the following order: 6 well-chopped anchovy fillets, ¼

130

cup finely chopped onions, 1 tablespoon finely chopped chives, 1 egg yolk, 2 turns of the pepper mill, a dash of Tabasco, ½ teaspoon Dijon mustard, 1 tablespoon or more capers, 1 tablespoon cognac.

Be sure all the ingredients are well blended. Taste for seasoning and add salt if necessary. Form into a loaf or a mound on a small bread board. Sprinkle with chopped parsley and refrigerate until ready to serve.

Marinated Mushrooms

RINSE and trim the stems from a pound of mushrooms. In a saucepan bring 1 quart salted water and the juice of 1 lemon to a boil, add the mushrooms and blanch for 2 minutes. Drain the mushrooms and transfer to a bowl. In another saucepan combine 1 cup tarragon vinegar, ⅓ cup olive oil, ¼ cup water, 4 sprigs parsley, 4 crushed peppercorns, 1 bay leaf, ½ teaspoon salt, and ¼ teaspoon each coriander and thyme. Bring the mixture to a boil and pour over the mushrooms. Allow to marinate 24 hours. When ready to serve, drain and transfer the mushrooms to a serving dish and garnish with a little chopped parsley.

Cucumbers in Sour Cream

PEEL and remove the seeds of three large cucumbers. Slice thinly, place in a shallow dish and add half of a thinly sliced onion. Marinate for a few hours in lemon juice, salt and pepper. Pour off the juices and gently toss with sour cream, adding the cream a tablespoon at a time. Adjust the seasoning and decorate with parsley or any minced green herb. Chill.

Guacamole Salad

MASH the meat of 3 ripe avocados, reserving the pits. Mix with 1 large peeled, seeded, and chopped tomato,

131

2 or 3 tablespoons chopped canned chilies, 1 minced sweet green pepper, and 2 tablespoons minced onion. Add 2 tablespoons olive oil, 1 tablespoon lemon juice, a scant ½ teaspoon sugar, and salt and pepper to taste. Return the avocado pits to the mixture—this will keep the avocados green—and refrigerate until ready to serve. Remove the pits to serve.

Assorted Breads

ON A large tray arrange thinly sliced French bread, thinly sliced black bread and rye. On the same tray place several rows of white toast, homemade. Cover the breads with plastic wrap until ready to serve. Place plates of unsalted butter on either side of the bread tray.

Strawberry Bavarois

CRUSH 4 cups of fresh strawberries and strain them through a fine sieve. Add 1 tablespoon lemon juice and ¾ cup sugar and stir until the sugar is completely dissolved. Soften 2 envelopes gelatin in ¼ cup water, dissolve it over hot water, and stir it into the purée. Fold in 2 cups stiffly whipped cream. Rinse a 2-quart mold in cold water, pour the strawberry cream into it, and chill thoroughly. This may also be prepared in individual molds. One half hour before serving, unmold, garnish with whole berries, and return to the refrigerator until ready to serve.

SHOPPING LIST

10 chicken legs
3-lb. veal rib roast
1½-lb. whole French or
    Italian sausage
1 lb. beef, round,
    sirloin, or tenderloin
1 bunch chives
1 lb. mushrooms
3 large cucumbers
3 ripe avocados
1 large tomato
1 sweet green pepper

4 cups ripe strawberries
small jar sour pickles
small jar sweet pickles
1 can anchovy fillets
small can hot chilies
assorted breads
unflavored gelatin
small jar capers
1 pt. heavy cream
4 oz. sour cream
cognac

STAPLES

parsley
garlic
Dijon mustard
flour
eggs
butter
onions
lemons
tarragon vinegar
olive oil
sugar
vegetable oil

tarragon
salt
pepper mill
peppercorns
bay leaf
Tabasco
coriander
thyme
mace
paprika

133

Tapenado with Eggplant and Red Caviar Garnish

Marinated Artichokes

Galantine of Veal

Sliced Breast of Turkey

Assorted Breads

Coeur à la Crème

TO SERVE 12

WINE
*French or domestic
Pouilly-Fumé or a fine
Sparkling Rosé*

REMARKS

T<small>HIS</small> is a more elegant, though slightly more complicated and time-consuming buffet. Again, it is designed to easily handle a lot of people at dinner. This menu also makes a lovely buffet lunch as well as a wonderful late evening buffet, where guests may not wish to eat too heavily.

METHOD

T<small>HE</small> tapenado and the turkey may be prepared the same day as the party. The galantine, marinated artichoke hearts, and coeur à la crème should be prepared at least 2 days ahead. Follow the method for the buffet arrangements on page 128.

Tapenado

I<small>NTO</small> the container of an electric blender, put 6 ounces pitted black olives, ½-ounce can flat anchovy fillets, 4 ounces tuna fish, 2 tablespoons capers, 1 tablespoon cognac, 3 tablespoons olive oil, 1 generous teaspoon dry mustard, and freshly ground pepper. Start the blender and dribble in up to ¼ cup more olive oil and up to ¼ cup more cognac. As soon as everything is completely mixed and has the texture of a coarse, spreadable paste, stop the blending. Check the seasoning and texture. If the spread is too thick, add more olive oil; if flavor is not sharp enough add more cognac and mustard.

Red Caviar Garnish

I<small>NTO</small> the container of an electric blender put the juice of 1 lemon, 3 tablespoons olive oil, 4 ounces salmon roe, and 1½ tablespoons tomato paste. Blend at medium high speed. The consistency of the mixture should be that of

135

a stiff mayonnaise. If it is not thick enough, add fresh bread crumbs, a tablespoon at a time. If too thick add more olive oil.

Eggplant Garnish

PRICK an eggplant with a fork in about a dozen places, rub with olive oil, and place in a baking dish in a preheated 400-degree oven. When the eggplant is tender, about 1 hour, remove from the oven, cut open and dig out pulp with a spoon. Put into a saucepan over medium heat. Mash down eggplant and stir continually to evaporate water and to thicken. Work in olive oil, spoon by spoon, the juice of a lemon, about a teaspoon of dried marjoram, plus salt and pepper to taste. When the mixture is about the consistency of mayonnaise, chill in the refrigerator. After it is chilled, check seasonings.

Arrange the tapenado with the 2 garnishes in separate dishes next to an attractively arranged platter of assorted raw vegetables. Some suggestions are cauliflower flowerets, carrot, celery, and zucchini sticks, radishes, etc. Serve plenty of thinly sliced French bread so that your guests may either dip the vegetables or spread the mixtures on the bread.

Marinated Artichokes

CUT off the tips and pull off the tough outer leaves from 24 artichoke hearts. Cut in half through the stem and wash well. In a heavy saucepan, mix 2 tablespoons cold water, ½ cup olive oil, and ¼ cup tarragon vinegar. Bring to a boil and add 2 whole bay leaves, ¼ teaspoon fennel seed, ½ teaspoon each thyme and coriander, 1 teaspoon salt, 12 peppercorns, and 3 or 4 sprigs of parsley. Simmer covered for 5 minutes. Then drop in the artichoke hearts, making sure there is enough liquid to cover. If not, add more oil, vinegar, etc. Cover. Continue simmering gently until artichokes are cooked through. Let cool and refrigerate.

Galantine of Veal

HAVE the butcher bone a breast of veal, reserving the bones. You will need a piece of meat about 12 inches long and 8 or 9 inches wide; it might be necessary to pound the meat to get the desired size. Lay the veal in a large container. Cut ½ pound smoked ham into ½-inch cubes and fit neatly around the veal. Sprinkle with salt, allspice, peppercorns, and, if desired, sliced truffles. Pour over ½ cup cognac and ½ cup Madeira wine. Cover tightly with foil and marinate about 5 hours. Grind finely ½ pound bacon and 1 pound veal. Mix with ¼ cup chopped parsley, 2 minced shallots, ½ teaspoon salt and pepper. Refrigerate until ready to stuff the veal.

When ready to stuff, place the veal slab, wiped dry, on a large double-thick piece of cheesecloth. Strain the marinating liquid into the ground meat mixture, add the marinated ham and truffles, and mix thoroughly. Place this stuffing down the center length of the veal slab, stopping about 2 inches from each end. Now roll up the veal carefully, wrap it tightly in cheesecloth, and tie it with string. It must be secure, as you do not want to lose the stuffing. Set the galantine in the bottom of a large heavy pot, pack around it the veal breast bones and a split veal knuckle. Add 2 leeks, 3 carrots, and 2 onions, all in chunks, 2 cloves of minced garlic, 2 teaspoons each marjoram and thyme, a few sprigs of parsley, 2 whole bay leaves, 12 whole peppercorns, ½ teaspoon mace, and ½ teaspoon sait. Pour in just enough chicken or veal stock and dry white wine to cover the galantine. Bring quickly to a boil, then turn heat down, cover, and simmer gently for 2½ hours. Turn off the heat and let cool in the stock.

Lift out the galantine and set it on a platter to drain. Weight it while it cools. Strain the liquid from the pot

137

and add ½ cup Madeira wine. This should cool into a firm jelly; if it is not quite firm enough, cook it more to reduce it. Finally, when the galantine is cool, remove the cheesecloth, place the galantine seam-side down in a mold, reheat the jelly, and pour over the galantine. Cover and refrigerate. Unmold and slice to serve.

Sliced Breast of Turkey

ROAST a 10-pound turkey according to your favorite method. Do not overcook, as the turkey will be dry. Let stand at least 2 hours. Carve the breast meat and arrange attractively on a platter. Sprinkle generously with salt, pepper, and finely minced parsley.

Assorted Breads

SEE page 132.

Coeur à la Crème

PRESS a pound of cottage cheese through a fine sieve and combine with 1 pound cream cheese and 2 cups heavy cream. Beat until smooth and season to taste with salt. Line a large heart-shaped basket with cheesecloth and fill it with the cheese. Stand the basket on a plate in the refrigerator for two days to drain off the whey. When ready to serve, unmold onto a platter and garnish the *coeur* with strawberries that have been sprinkled with sugar. Individual heart molds may also be used.

SHOPPING LIST

1 breast of veal, boned
bones from the veal
    breast
split veal knuckle
1 lb. ground veal
½ lb. smoked ham
½ lb. ground bacon
10-lb. turkey,
    large-breasted
8 oz. fresh black olives
4-oz. can tuna
½-oz. can anchovy
    fillets
small jar capers
4-oz. jar salmon roe
1 or 2 cans truffles
    (optional)

small can tomato paste
1 lb. cottage cheese
1 lb. cream cheese
1 pt. heavy cream
1 eggplant
assorted raw vegetables
    for tapenado
24 fresh artichoke hearts
2 shallots
2 pts. ripe strawberries
2 leeks
3 carrots
assorted breads
cognac
dry white wine
Madeira wine

STAPLES

olive oil
lemons
tarragon vinegar
parsley
onions
garlic
chicken or
    veal stock

dry mustard
bay leaves
fennel seed
thyme
coriander
salt
peppercorns
allspice
marjoram
mace

139

Dinners from Normandy

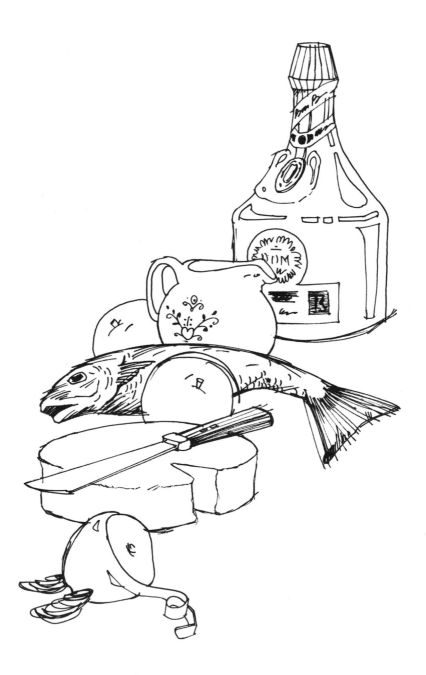

Cheese Soufflé

Poisson Braisé à la Dieppoise

(Fish Braised Dieppe Style)

Carottes Vichy

Pommes Rissolées

Tarte aux Pommes à la M. Lecourt

(M. Lecourt's Apple Tart)

TO SERVE 6

WINE
*California Pinot Blanc or
Folle Blanche, Chilean
Riesling or German
Bernkasteler*

REMARKS

THIS menu and the two following were created after a delightful time I spent in Dieppe on the French coast of Normandy. While I was there I attended classes in Norman cooking, offered by the charming M. Lecourt, former chef-owner of a well-known restaurant near Rouen. The cheese soufflé and fish are from his classes. He was kind enough to share with me his unusual apple tart recipe, which is his own invention, as is the method for browning pastry crusts used throughout this book. So, a delicious and typically Norman menu.

METHOD

EVERY dish may be prepared in advance. For the cheese soufflé, follow the method for salmon soufflé, page 87. The fish may be finished, kept warm, and the sauce reheated just before serving. Finish cooking and reheat the carrots and potatoes. Be certain not to overcook the custard on M. Lecourt's tart. An impressive method of serving the main dish is to place the fish in the middle of a large serving tray. Surround it with the carrots and potatoes, garnish with minced parsley, and bring it to the table.

Cheese Soufflé

IN A heavy saucepan, melt 2 tablespoons butter, stir in 2 tablespoons flour, and cook 2 minutes over a medium flame. Add ¾ cup warmed milk. Turn to a low flame and cook an additional 5 minutes until the sauce thickens. Season with salt and cayenne pepper and 1 teaspoon Dijon mustard. Remove from the heat and add 3 egg yolks alternately with a generous cup of shredded imported Swiss or Gruyère cheese. Return to stove, melting the cheese

144

over a low heat and stirring constantly. This much may be done well ahead. Twenty minutes before serving, fold in 5 stiffly beaten egg whites and pour into a generously buttered soufflé dish. Bake in a 400-degree oven 20 to 25 minutes. Serve immediately.

Poisson Braisé à la Dieppoise

(Fish Braised Dieppe Style)

Butter generously a flat ovenproof dish. Sprinkle with 3 tablespoons finely chopped shallots. Place a 3½-pound whole firm-fleshed white fish or 3 pounds of firm fish fillets on top of the shallots; season with salt and cayenne pepper and pour enough dry white wine over the fish to barely cover. Press a buttered wax paper over the fish and place in a 375-degree oven for approximately 20 minutes. If using a whole fish, turn after 10 minutes. Be careful not to overcook. When the fish is done, remove from the pan and keep it warm. If a whole fish is used, remove the bones and skin at this point. Reduce the braising liquid left in the pan by half, using a medium heat, and add 6 or more generous tablespoons crème fraîche (see page 160). Allow the sauce to boil down to the consistency of thick heavy cream. Add a cup of raw mussels or Olympia oysters and a cup of tiny cooked shrimp. When ready to serve, reheat the sauce gently and spoon over the fish. Garnish with a little chopped parsley.

Carottes Vichy

Cook 2 dozen tiny peeled whole carrots uncovered in boiling Vichy water to which a teaspoon of sugar and a tablespoon of butter have been added. When the carrots are tender, drain if any liquid remains. Add a generous amount of butter, season with salt and white pepper, and sprinkle with finely chopped parsley. If baby carrots are not available, buy the smallest carrots and trim them to the size of baby carrots.

145

Pommes Rissolées

Scrub and place in a saucepan 18 tiny red potatoes. Add water to cover, a little salt, and bring to a boil. Boil for 3 minutes. Drain, melt 4 tablespoons butter in an oven-proof dish, add the potatoes, and roast in a 350-degree oven until tender. Sprinkle with salt and pepper. If small red potatoes are not available, cut larger potatoes into balls.

Tarte aux Pommes à la M. Lecourt
(M. Lecourt's Apple Tart)

Roll out a tart pastry (page 163) and line a well-buttered 8-inch tart pan or flan ring. Peel 3 Pippin or other tart green apples and slice in ¼-inch-thick slices. Arrange in overlapping circles, one layer deep, over pastry on the

bottom of the pan. Beat 2 eggs, add 2 heaped tablespoons sugar and 5 heaped tablespoons crème fraîche (see page 160). Mix well and add 2 tablespoons Calvados. Pour the custard over the apples. Preheat the oven to 425 degrees and put the tart on the floor of a gas oven for 10 minutes or over the coils on top of an electric stove for 7 minutes, in order to brown the bottom crust. Then lower the oven to 350 degrees and place the tart on the oven rack for an additional 10 or 15 minutes until the pastry is browned and the custard set.

146

SHOPPING LIST

3½-lb. whole white fish *or*
   3 lbs. white fish fillets
   enough mussels to make
      a cup shelled *or*
   8 oz. Olympia oysters
   6 oz. tiny cooked
      shrimp
   8 oz. imported Swiss or
      Gruyère cheese

   3 shallots
   2 doz. tiny carrots
   4 tart green apples
  18 small red potatoes
   ½ pint heavy cream
   4 oz. sour cream
   dry white wine
   Calvados

STAPLES

butter
flour
milk
Dijon mustard
eggs

parsley
sugar

salt
cayenne pepper

Soupe de Poisson

(Fish Soup)

Côtes de Porc Farcie de M. Jean Tilquin

(M. Jean Tilquin's Stuffed Pork Chop)

Potatoes Clemenceau

Butter Lettuce and Parsley Salad

Tarte Normande

WINE
*From Bordeaux, a Pomerol, or
a good Grignolino from
California.*

EVEN though Norman cooking is a provincial style of cookery, it is extraordinarily subtle and delicate. The clear fish soup in this menu is so subtly seasoned that I was unable to identify the saffron when I first tasted it. The stuffed pork chop is an invention of M. Jean Tilquin, chef-owner of the Hotel d'Univers in Dieppe. It is the most delicious way I know of preparing pork chops. Another apple tart, typically Norman, is a part of this menu.

THE tart should be prepared in advance and allowed to cool to room temperature. The soup can be finished and reheated before serving. The pork chops keep nicely for several hours and need only be reheated in their sauce just before dinner. The potatoes, mushrooms and peas may also be prepared ahead and reheated. My favorite way of serving the main course is to place the pork chops down the center of a large serving platter surrounded by the potatoes and vegetables. Sprinkle the chops with minced parsley, bring the platter to the table, and serve.

Soupe de Poisson
(Fish Soup)

CLEAN well and cut into cubes the white parts of 4 leeks. Sauté over a low flame for 5 minutes in 1 tablespoon butter and 1 tablespoon vegetable oil. Add 2 cloves of garlic cut in half, a teaspoon or more of dried thyme, a bay leaf, and 4 medium tomatoes, cut in quarters. Add 3 pounds of white fish, skin, bones and all, cut into pieces, and cover with cold water. Add ¼ teaspoon saffron and ½ teaspoon sugar. Bring to a boil, cover and simmer 40 minutes. Pour the soup through a fine sieve, pressing down hard on the fish and vegetables to extract all the flavors. Strain once again to make certain the broth is perfectly clear. Return the soup to the pot, taste for seasonings, and add salt, white pepper, and more saffron if desired. Simmer uncovered until the broth is cooked down to a rich flavor. Serve with freshly made croutons.

Croutons

CUT off the crusts from 4 thinly sliced pieces of white bread. Cut into small dice and sauté in hot butter until golden brown. Remove with a slotted spoon and drain on paper towels.

Côtes de Porc Farcie de M. Jean Tilquin
(M. Jean Tilquin's Stuffed Pork Chops)

SLIT eight 1¼-inch-thick center-cut pork chops to the bone. Sprinkle the opened chop with salt and pepper, spread generously with fresh or dried sage; place a thin slice of boiled ham and a slice of imported Gruyère cheese in the opening and close the chop. Season the outside lightly with salt and pepper. Melt 3 tablespoons butter in a large heavy skillet and sauté the chops, covered, over low heat, 10 minutes for each side. Remove to a serving

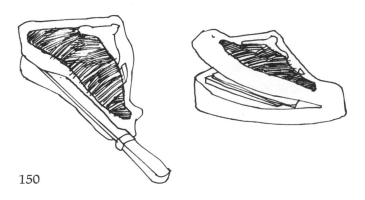

dish and keep warm. Pour out any excess fat remaining in the pan and add ½ cup dry white wine and ½ cup chicken or veal stock. Reduce rapidly over a high flame, taste for seasoning, and when ready to serve, spoon the sauce over each chop. Note: Do not overstuff the chops or the cheese will run out while cooking.

Potatoes Clemenceau

PEEL and cut 2 pounds potatoes into small uniform dice and fry them in clarified butter (see page 159) until tender. Combine the potatoes with a scant ½ pound thinly sliced mushrooms that have been sautéed in butter for 1 minute. Add 1 cup fresh green peas, barely cooked until tender (the Paul Mayer method, page 159), and drained. Season with salt and pepper to taste.

Tarte Normande

ROLL out a tart pastry (page 163) and line a well-buttered 8-inch tart pan or flan ring. Peel 4 tart apples, cut into quarters, and put them into a heavy saucepan with a tablespoon of water and 3 tablespoons finely granulated sugar. Cook until soft, press through a sieve, and cool. Cover the bottom of the tart pastry with the apple sauce, about ½ inch thick, and then cover with thin slices of apple, arranged in overlapping circles. Preheat the oven to 425 degrees and put the tart on the bottom of a gas oven for 10 minutes or over the coils on top of an electric stove for 7 minutes, in order to brown the lower crust. Then lower the oven to 350 degrees and place the tart on the oven rack for an additional 10 or 15 minutes until the pastry is browned. Glaze with apricot jam diluted with a little water and boiled until thick, or cover immediately after baking with powdered sugar.

151

SHOPPING LIST

3 lbs. white fish, skin and bones
8 1¼-inch-thick center-cut pork chops
8 thin slices boiled ham
8 thin slices imported Gruyère cheese
4 leeks

4 tomatoes
½ lb. mushrooms
8 tart green apples
1 lb. fresh green peas
thin-sliced white bread
apricot jam
dry white wine

STAPLES

butter (1 lb.)
vegetable oil
garlic
sugar
chicken or veal stock
potatoes (2 lbs.)
flour
eggs
powdered sugar

thyme
bay leaf
saffron
salt
black pepper
white pepper
sage

Scallops au Naturel

Poulet Vallée d'Auge
(Chicken Normandy Style)

Green Beans with Parsley

Cottage-Fried Potatoes

Salad

Benedictine Soufflé

REMARKS

DIEPPE's fishing fleet supplies over half the scallops to France; consequently scallops are served frequently in Dieppe. The scallops offered on this menu are prepared in the very simplest and, I think, most elegant manner. The chicken is typically Norman, using both Calvados and cream. The soufflé is made from Benedictine, a liquor distilled in Normandy.

METHOD

THE chicken and sauce may be prepared ahead and held separately, the sauce to be reheated slowly and spooned over the chicken just before serving. Both the green beans and the potatoes also reheat nicely. Have the scallops washed and waiting next to a heavy skillet with melted butter. Should you decide to serve them as an hors d'oeuvre, midway into the cocktail hour, flour and sauté the scallops quickly. Spoon into waiting scallop shells, sprinkle with parsley, put a small wedge of lemon on the side and serve immediately. For the soufflé, follow the method on page 161.

Scallops au Naturel

WASH 1½ pounds scallops, removing any bits of shell or black threads. Dry them well, season with salt and pepper, and roll lightly in flour. Melt 5 tablespoons butter in a heavy skillet and sauté the scallops over a medium flame 2 or 3 minutes each side. They should be a nice golden color. Do not overcook or they will become tough. Serve in scallop shells. If necessary, melt more butter to pour over the scallops. Garnish with chopped parsley and thinly sliced lemons.

154

Poulet Vallée d'Auge
(Chicken Normandy Style)

CUT two 2-pound chickens into 6 pieces each. (Reserve the innards, wing tips, and backs for the stock pot.) Season with salt and pepper and sauté in a heavy deep skillet in plenty of hot butter until golden brown on both sides. Remove the chicken and add 1 pound finely sliced mushrooms and 3 finely minced shallots. Cook about a minute, tossing frequently, and return the chicken to the pot. Flame the chicken with ½ cup or more Calvados. After the flame dies, add a bay leaf and a teaspoon each of thyme and parsley. Cover the pot and cook approximately 15 minutes more or until done. Take the chicken out, put into a serving dish and keep warm. Add 8 tablespoons of crème fraîche (see page 160) to the juices remaining and cook the sauce down to the consistency of heavy cream. Season with salt and pepper to taste. Spoon the sauce over the chicken and serve.

Green Beans with Parsley

CUT 2 pounds fresh green beans into 1-inch lengths and cook them in chicken stock, using the Paul Mayer Method (see page 159), until just barely tender. Drain, and toss the beans with ⅓ cup each of melted butter and minced parsley and 2 tablespoons fresh lemon juice. Salt and pepper to taste.

Cottage-Fried Potatoes

SLICE 6 hot, freshly boiled potatoes and brown them quickly in chicken fat or bacon drippings. Season with salt and pepper.

Salad

A BUTTER lettuce and parsley salad is suggested (see pages 162–163).

Benedictine Soufflé

IN A medium-sized heavy saucepan, melt 3 tablespoons butter. Remove the pan from the fire, add 2 tablespoons flour, blend well, and return the pan to the heat. Continue cooking the butter-flour mixture until it bubbles slightly. Remove from the heat and blend in ¾ cup hot milk. Place the pan over the flame and stir until the sauce becomes very thick and boils. Stir it for 5 minutes, from the beginning of the boiling. Then remove from the heat and rapidly stir in 5 egg yolks that have been beaten with 3 tablespoons sugar. Add 6 tablespoons Benedictine. Whisk 6 egg whites until they are stiff but not dry, add 2 teaspoons sugar, and continue beating for another 30 seconds. Carefully fold the whites into the base and fill a prepared soufflé dish (page 161) with the mixture. Bake in a 400-degree oven for 20 to 25 minutes. Remove from the oven, take off the paper collar, and serve immediately.

SHOPPING LIST

1½ lbs. scallops	¼ pt. sour cream
2 2-lb. chickens	½ pt. heavy cream
1 lb. mushrooms	2 heads butter lettuce
2 lbs. fresh green beans	Calvados
3 shallots	Benedictine

STAPLES

butter	chicken fat (¼ cup)
parsley	vegetable oil
chicken stock	tarragon vinegar
lemons	
eggs (7)	salt
flour	pepper
milk	bay leaf
potatoes (6)	thyme
sugar	

Equivalents

a pinch or a dash	slightly less than ⅛ teaspoon
3 teaspoons	1 tablespoon
4 tablespoons	¼ cup
5 tablespoons	⅓ cup less 1 tablespoon
8 tablespoons	½ cup
12 tablespoons	¾ cup
16 tablespoons	1 cup
2 tablespoons	1 liquid ounce
1 cup	½ pint
4 cups flour	1 pound
2 cups liquid	16 fluid ounces
4 cups liquid	1 quart
5 large eggs	1 cup
8 egg whites	1 cup
12–15 egg yolks	1 cup
¼ pound (stick) butter	½ cup
1 cup butter	½ pound
2 cups grated cheese	½ pound
¼ cup lemon juice	1 large lemon

Basic Recipes

Beef Stock

INTO a large soup kettle, put 3 pounds beef shank and 2 pounds cracked beef bones. Add 4 leeks, 2 stalks celery (leaves and all), 3 carrots, a large onion, 3 sprigs of parsley and any other uncooked vegetables you might have. Add a teaspoon of salt, a bay leaf and a bouquet garni (see below). Add water to cover, bring to a boil, lower the heat, skim off the foam, and simmer, partially covered, for 3 to 4 hours. Taste the stock. If the flavor is strong, it is ready; otherwise, simmer uncovered until the flavor is good and strong. Cool, strain through a fine sieve, and refrigerate. When cool, the fat can easily be removed. The stock is now ready to be used or can be stored in the freezer for several months.

Beurre Manié

CREAM together, with your fingers, butter and flour in proportions of 1 teaspoon butter to 1 teaspoon flour. Be sure that the flour and butter are completely incorporated. If the beurre manié is not to be used immediately, roll into little balls and refrigerate, to be used as needed.

Bouquet Garni

BOUQUET garni is the French term for a bundle of vegetables and herbs of your own choice or as specified in the recipe, tied together with string for easy removal. If you use all dried herbs, tie them into a little bundle of cheesecloth. A fresh bouquet garni might include a small celery stalk with leaves, a sprig of parsley, a bay leaf, and a sprig of thyme. Use vegetables and herbs in bouquets garnis as desired or as specified.

Chicken or Duck Stock

THE same as beef stock, substituting a 3- or 4-pound stewing hen or duck with giblets, or an equal amount of discarded parts, such as wing tips, backs, necks, and giblets. Do not use the liver.

Clarified Butter

MELT any desired amount of unsalted butter slowly over low heat in a heavy saucepan. When the last of the butter is melted, remove from the heat and carefully skim off the foam with a spoon. Strain the pure yellow oil through a fine sieve into a container, being certain to leave all the milky residue in the bottom of the pan. This pure oil, or "clarified butter," may be stored in the freezer for months. Clarified butter is used to brown delicate meats such as veal, lamb, or chicken quickly over a very high heat. It will not burn.

Cooking Green Vegetables by the Paul Mayer Method

THE following method of cooking green vegetables is the one I have found to give the greenest, most tender results. It is called the Paul Mayer Method after its inventor, a former cooking teacher of mine, Paul Mayer of San Francisco. Place a heaping teaspoon of sugar in a heavy saucepan. Add the cleaned green vegetables and turn the flame on high. When the sugar melts, pour rapidly boiling water into the pot to just cover the vegetables. Add salt.

Cover immediately and boil until the desired degree of doneness is reached. I use a toothpick to determine this. Salt and pepper to taste.

Crème Fraîche

CRÈME FRAÎCHE is an approximation of the fresh heavy cream of France. Combine well 1 cup heavy cream and ½ cup sour cream in a small saucepan. Put over a very low flame, stirring constantly until just barely warm. Remove immediately, pour into a glass bowl, and place in the refrigerator uncovered for several hours. The result is a thick cream that will not curdle in a sauce. Sweetened, it is delicious over fruit. It keeps well if refrigerated, for about a week.

Crêpes

PUT the following into the container of a blender: 2 eggs and ¾ cup milk. Add ½ cup plus 1 tablespoon of flour, 1 teaspoon oil, and a pinch of salt. Combine in the blender for a few seconds. Allow the resulting batter to stand an hour or more. When you are ready to make the crêpes, heat a crêpe pan, grease it with a little unsalted butter (this is only necessary for the first one), and pour in just enough batter to cover the bottom of the pan. If you pour in too much, just pour the batter back immediately, before it has time to set. The crêpes must be paper thin. Cook over a moderate flame until the bottom begins to brown and the top is dry. You may turn and barely brown the other side if you wish, although it is unnecessary. Stack the crêpes on a board and cover with a cloth. If they are not to be used within a few hours, they may be frozen. The above recipe makes about twelve 7-inch or sixteen 5-inch crêpes.

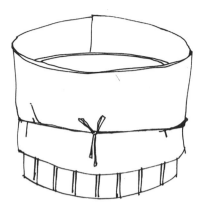

Dessert Soufflé Dish Preparation

DESSERT soufflés require a "collar" or band of buttered wax paper tied around the dish extending above the rim to prevent the soufflé from spilling over before it has a chance to set. This is done only with dessert soufflés as they are generally lighter in texture than savory soufflés, therefore rising more quickly and taking longer to set. Butter the soufflé dish well and sprinkle with sugar, tilting the dish to make sure the interior is well coated. Then cut a piece of wax paper that will go around the dish, fold it in half lengthwise and butter, but do not sugar, this collar. Arrange it around the soufflé dish, buttered side in, and tie with a single piece of kitchen string. This may be prepared several hours ahead.

Dinner Salads

I LIKE a dinner salad served after the main course. It is refreshing, especially after a rich dinner and seems to serve as a perfect transition to dessert. The dinner salad should never be more than a combination of complementary lettuces with a light vinaigrette sauce. The follow-

161

ing preparation is necessary. Wash, dry well, and place in paper towels, and then a plastic bag, any desired amount of salad greens. Crisp in the refrigerator. A half hour before your guests arrive, tear enough leaves to make small salads for each guest, and put into a large (I prefer wooden) salad bowl. The bowl must be large enough to allow for tossing. Put the salad, bowl and all, back into the refrigerator to chill until ready to serve. Toss with the dressing at the dinner table or in the kitchen and serve immediately. Following are some recommended salad combinations.

Butter lettuce and minced parsley with an herbed dressing (see below).

Watercress and endive, together or alone, with a mustard dressing (page 163).

Romaine lettuce, with an oil and vinegar dressing (page 163).

Salad Dressings

THE kind of oil used for salad dressing is a matter of personal taste. I prefer a light vegetable or walnut oil and always use the finest quality wine vinegars available. When tossing a salad, don't pour on too much dressing. Start with two tablespoons—you can always add more. Toss gently with two long-handled spoons or forks and taste a leaf in order to judge whether or not there is enough dressing coating the leaves. Combine the following ingredients for

Herbed Dressing

5 tablespoons oil
2½ tablespoons herbed white wine vinegar (tarragon, basil, oregano, thyme, etc.)
¼ teaspoon salt or to taste
¼ teaspoon pepper or to taste

Oil and Vinegar Dressing

5 tablespoons oil
2½ tablespoons red
   wine vinegar
¼ teaspoon sugar

¼ teaspoon salt or to
   taste
¼ teaspoon pepper or to
   taste

Mustard Dressing

5 tablespoons oil
2½ tablespoons white
   wine vinegar

1 teaspoon or more
   Dijon mustard
¼ teaspoon salt
¼ teaspoon pepper

Sour Cream Pastry

Sift 2¼ cups flour and 1 teaspoon salt together into a large chilled bowl. Drop 6 ounces chilled unsalted butter, cut into ¼-inch bits, into the bowl. Working quickly, rub the flour and butter together until you have a coarse, crumbly mixture. Mix together 1 egg and ½ cup sour cream and combine with the flour-butter mixture until you have a soft pliable ball. Wrap in wax paper and chill about an hour before rolling out.

Tart Pastry

On a pastry board pile 1¾ cups sifted flour. Make a well in the center, and place in it 5 ounces chilled unsalted butter, cut into ¼-inch bits, 2 tablespoons finely granulated sugar, a pinch of salt, and 2 egg yolks. With the tips of the fingers of one hand, quickly and lightly cream the butter, sugar, and egg yolks. Add a teaspoon or slightly more of ice water and blend flour into the creamed mixture. Shape into a ball and refrigerate for at least 1 hour before rolling out.

163

Tomato Sauce

MELT 1 tablespoon butter in a saucepan and add 1 clove of garlic which has been crushed through the garlic press, 1 small can of tomato paste, a 1-pound can of peeled Italian tomatoes, chopped coarsely, ½ teaspoon sugar, and salt, pepper, and basil to taste. Cook uncovered until thickened.

Veal Stock

THE same as beef stock, substituting veal shanks and knuckles for beef.

Recipe Index

Soups

Salads and Vegetables

Fish

Poultry

Meats

Desserts

Breads

Miscellaneous